FOR
WINE-LOVERS AND GOURMETS

By P. Morton Shand

A BOOK OF FRENCH WINE
A BOOK OF OTHER WINES THAN FRENCH
A BOOK OF FOOD

By Charles Walter Berry

VINIANA

By G. B. Stern

BOUQUET

By A. H. Adair

DINNERS LONG AND SHORT

THESE ARE BORZOI BOOKS PUBLISHED BY
ALFRED A. KNOPF

AMERICAN WINES

AND HOW TO MAKE THEM

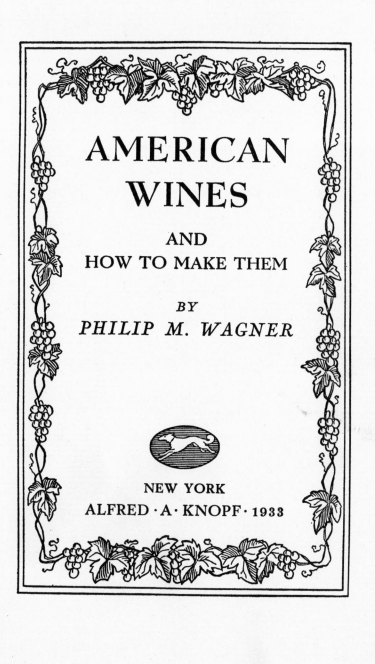

AMERICAN
WINES

AND
HOW TO MAKE THEM

BY
PHILIP M. WAGNER

NEW YORK
ALFRED · A · KNOPF · 1933

663
W

PUBLISHED SEPTEMBER I, 1933
SECOND PRINTING SEPTEMBER, 1933
THIRD PRINTING OCTOBER, 1933

PREFACE

WINE has enjoyed increasing popularity throughout the period of prohibition. I have even heard it suggested that if prohibition were to continue in force for another decade, we might reasonably expect the United States to become a wine-drinking nation. For this paradox we must thank our legislators, who with wisdom and humanity have permitted the making of naturally fermented fruit juices in the home, without unpleasant legal consequences, and so have helped to temper the rigours of an unsuccessful experiment.

But unfortunately the growth of domestic wine-making has taken place without any great increase of enlightenment as to proper wine-making methods. In Europe both peasants and proprietors of great estates make their own wine and are proud to serve it, and as a consequence the rules of sound wine-making are everybody's property. We have no such wine-making tradition. And the literature of œnology, in English, is woefully inadequate and for the most part buried in government publications which have been long out of print. Therefore much of our " home-made "

1994

wine is bad, when it need not be. My purpose in writing this book is to lay before the domestic winemaker the elements of the art. The book is in no sense original. I have been content to follow my betters and have with strict determination spurned the allurements of novelty. Originality in wine-making, save by a Pasteur, is always suspect. If in spite of my resolution some traces of it have crept in, I can only offer my apologies in advance and ask the indulgent reader to point them out to me. Perhaps I shall have some future opportunity to make amends.

A word or two as to the plan of the book. The first three chapters are historical and descriptive. The ruthlessly practical may skip them, though I hope they won't, for I have been at some little pains in writing them to strike a just and pleasing balance between instruction and diversion. If they are firmly intent on learning the how without regard to the why, they may also skip Chapter iv, but again I shall be disappointed, for that chapter contains a good deal of curious information that was not lightly come by. I am not unmindful, however, that the ruthlessly practical must be served; and for their convenience I have even devised a synopsis of wine-making, which is printed at the end of the book and in which the bare bones of the art are displayed without any flesh on them at all.

I cannot conclude this preface without mentioning my obligation to Mr. Hamilton Owens, my companion in many pleasant œnological experiments, whose ready sympathy and keen critical perceptions

Preface

have been my constant support; and to my wife, Helen D. Wagner, the silent partner in the writing of this book. I want also to thank Mr. H. L. Mencken for his interest in it and for permission to reprint the parts of Chapters ii and iii which appeared originally in the *American Mercury*, Mr. August W. Derleth, of Sauk City, Wisconsin, Mr. F. E. Gladwin, of Fredonia, New York, Mr. H. F. Stoll, of San Francisco, and the Gentlemen of the Bureau of Chemistry and Soils, Department of Agriculture. I must also thank the Association of Official Agricultural Chemists for permission to include material from the latest edition of *Official and Tentative Methods of Analysis, A. O. A. C.*

The writing of this handbook has been the pleasantest sort of recreation for me, and if it introduces some people to the twin pleasures of wine-making and wine-drinking and helps some of those who already know these pleasures, I shall be adequately rewarded.

P. M. W.

Riderwood, Maryland,
May 23, 1933

CONTENTS

AMERICAN WINES

AND HOW TO MAKE THEM

Chapter One

ON GRAPES AND WINE

THE WORD "wine" is of such grand antiquity and has so often been the victim of licence, poetic and other, that it is necessary at the very beginning to identify and dispose of certain popular fancies and to say just what wine is and what it is not. Wine is not a stupefying drug or poison, to be compared with hashish, cocaine, and the marihuana weed, despite the opinion of many earnest and well-meaning persons. It is but distantly related to the Demon Rum and the John Barleycorn of the diurnal press. The word is not a generic term for all beverages containing alcohol, as one might suppose from reading the minor poets of the late nineteenth century ("I cried for madder music and for stronger wine"). Wine is not, though it is often so used, a name for the naturally fermented juices of the blackberry, the strawberry, the apple, the pear, the currant, the cowslip, the dandelion, the damson, the quince, and the wild gooseberry; it has to serve duty for a sufficient variety of things without being applied to these. Nor — a thousand times nor — is it properly used in the name of a

3]

patented or proprietary compound, such as the " non-alcoholic ginger wine " which is admired by certain Englishmen, a beverage which is not non-alcoholic (since it contains a small percentage of alcohol), is not ginger (since its ginger flavouring is synthetic), and is not wine (simply because it is not wine).

Wine is the naturally fermented juice of the grape. At its best, wine is a delight to all of the senses except that of hearing — and even, on some occasions, a delight to that. At its worst it is undrinkable. None have enumerated the properties of a good wine with more pleasing succinctness than the elder Pliny, who wrote: " Wine refreshes the stomach, sharpens the appetite, blunts care and sadness, and conduces to slumber." But sound or bad, fine or merely ordinary, sparkling, fortified, or dry, it is the child of the vine and of nothing else. Unless the parentage be beyond all cavil, it is not wine.

Wine is called either white or red. Yet those two small, blunt words cover an infinity of gradations, as the colours of the spectrum flow without break from one into the next. A red wine, at one extreme, may be an inky purple, like the new wines made from the Petite Sirah of our Pacific Coast. With that as one extreme, we find red wines extending through every slightest degree from purple into a deep magenta, from there into ruby-red, to deep carmine, and finally to rose. Further, in addition to its peculiar " original " colour, a red wine undergoes a constant change, as, with age, some portion of its pigment is thrown down

as sediment, until finally it attains that pale tawny
" onion-skin " redness of extreme old age.

There are as many gradations in the colour of white
wine. Some white wines are almost literally without
colour. Some are the colour of bleached straw, and
some, such as the wines made from our native Delawares or some of the light white wines of France,
have even a faint suggestion of green. Others are
straw with a bias toward the yellows; and so we come
down through shades of bright gold, of amber, of
topaz, to those which are brownish, whether by
nature, like the wines made from certain varieties of
grapes, by design, like certain brown sherries, or by
accident, as when a sensitive or sickly white wine is
exposed to oxidation by the air. Then there are the
curious bastard wines, the *vins rosés* and the *vins gris*
or *tachés*, which are neither white wines nor red, but,
like coloured etchings and Kipling's Indo-Europeans,
are the unhappy objects of suspicion and contempt.

But wines have to be divided according to another
character than that of colour. Wines may be still or
sparkling.

The pattern of all sparkling wines is Champagne,
a wine which many suppose to be the favourite
beverage of the idle rich, particularly the subdivision
of that class which is known as " wasters," being
served always in frosty silver buckets and drunk by
the wasters in question from large goblets of gleam-
ing crystal, or, better, from the slippers of voluptuous
temptresses. The moving pictures have strengthened

5]

this supposition. Actually, Champagne is an effervescent wine made according to a special and very exacting method from certain grapes which are grown on the slopes of the Mountain of Reims,[1] which rises between the valleys of the Vesle and the Marne in the northeastern part of France. This wine owes its peculiar quality to the discovery of a monk, Dom Pérignon of the Abbey of Hautvillers, who noticed that if a wine is bottled and tightly corked before it has quite finished its fermentation, the gas which is a normal product of fermentation will dissolve in the wine and be released as bubbles when the bottle is later opened. The popularity of these effervescent, or sparkling, wines became so great that the Champagne district failed utterly to meet the demand; the consequence is that every wine-growing region of the world, including the United States under prohibition, now makes its " champagne," much of it from grapes hopelessly ill-suited to the purpose. Sometimes the sparkle is induced by the natural method of Dom Pérignon, and sometimes by the less subtle method of pumping the sparkle into it, as the sparkle is pumped into pop and cheap beer.

Still wines are those which do not sparkle, being content merely to glow. It is these that comprise the bulk of the world's wines; among them are found the finest and most famous of them all, and also the ordinary wholesome, nutritious beverage wines which are for many people as much a part of their existence as the air they breathe and the food they eat.

[1] Actually not a mountain at all, but a table-land.

On Grapes and Wine

Of still wines there are several categories. There are the fortified wines, of which those produced on the Iberian Peninsula, the sherries of Spain and the ports of Portugal, are the most celebrated, the most popular, and the most largely imitated. These are in no sense beverage wines, but should be looked upon rather as liqueurs, being always too rich in alcohol for unmeasured drinking and frequently sweet into the bargain. They are made by the normal fermentation of the grape; but they differ from other wines in that, at the conclusion of fermentation, they are fortified by the addition of grape brandy.[1] Port and sherry are therefore wines to be drunk with discretion and even circumspection, wines to be sipped rather than swallowed — wines suited, in a word, to the conclusion of a good meal, when the appetites have ceased their clamour and the mood is one for more deliberate appreciation. Port and sherry were for long the favourite wines of Great Britain and, indeed, are popular wherever the climate is damp and clammy. It was not until the passage of the enlightened Gladstone Act, which based duties not on bulk but on the degree of alcoholic content and so favoured the lighter wines, that the supremacy of port was seriously challenged in England. Needless to say, fortified wines are no longer made only in Spain and Portugal, but are produced in nearly every wine-growing country. Almost the only wines freely available to Americans during prohibition have been the highly

[1] There are, it is true, certain light, dry sherries which are unfortified.

alcoholic port and sherry "tonics" which are sold without limit in every drug-store.

The sweet and liquorous but unfortified dessert wines are also to be classed among the still wines. These wines are fermented naturally from grapes so rich in sugar that the fermentation comes to a stop before all of the sugar has been converted into alcohol. They are too alcoholic to be drunk freely, and their cloying sweetness is another barrier to their free use. They are, definitely, wines of special purpose, to be drunk only at the conclusion of a meal. The most famous of them are probably the white Sauternes, and of the Sauternes the most famous is the wine of Château Yquem. Some of the sweet wines, such as the Muscats which have been so popular in the United States during prohibition, are made from grapes which at their peak of ripeness are excessively rich in sugar. Others are made from grapes which have been allowed to hang on the vines until they are over-ripe and some of the moisture of the grapes has been lost by evaporation. Such are the Sauternes, the celebrated Tokay *essence* of Hungary, and certain of the *Auslese* wines of the Rhine and the Moselle. The cheaper wines of this type are sometimes made by the artificial condensation of the must before the fermentation is begun; this method was very popular in California.

Then there is the small and relatively unimportant group of wines which are not really wines at all. Characteristic members of this family are the *mistelles* of France, the Portuguese Geropigas, and the pre-prohibition angelicas of California. These are made

[8

by what is known as *mutage*, which is merely the addition of brandy or alcohol to the fresh juice in sufficient quantity to stop fermentation before it ever has a chance to begin. The characteristics of these are therefore not the characteristics of honest wine, but of fresh grape juice. As much as thirty per cent of alcohol frequently lurks behind the innocent aroma of fresh grapes. Strangely enough, these angelicas have always been looked upon as being " for the ladies," though a lady must be very much a lady not to disclose the effect of a glass or two.

Finally we come to the dry natural wines, with which, save for these preliminary skirmishes and reconnoitres, this book is concerned. Sweet wines, sparkling wines, ports, and sherries all have their unquestioned uses, their impassioned advocates, and their indubitable virtues. But the wine-drinkers of the world owe and acknowledge their first allegiance to the dry natural wines, red and white. These are the wines of which Pliny spoke, refreshing as nothing else, guardians against care and sadness, innocent and companionable friends of man since the miracle of fermentation was first vouchsafed unto him; and with religion — for the two have always been linked together — one of the two great consolations for a life which Hobbes all too accurately described as " solitary, poor, nasty, brutish and short." The dry, natural wines — " light wines " if you will — are, first of all, cheap and wholesome beverages, gently stimulating and conducive to one's physical well-being. Every truly wine-drinking culture is erected upon the firm and ample base of these unpretentious wines. Some natural wines are capable of yielding profound æsthetic satisfaction, and to read of wine one might suppose that those are the only wines worth talking of or drinking. Yet their production is infinitesimal as compared to the bulk of the world's wine, and in a sense incidental, and they ought logically to follow, rather than to precede, in discussion as they do in life, the less pretentious but infinitely more important common wines. Language is a humble and useful vehicle of communication; great works of literature are the peaks rising above the plain and can have no meaning without reference to the plain. Great wines hold much the same relation to the ordinary wines; they cannot be understood and appreciated save by the person who knows and values the humbler virtues of the ordinary.

2

The history of wine is the history of the vine. Where the vine is cultivated, there also wine is its chief product and, as André Simon says, the most suitable and usually the cheapest beverage obtainable. This is a truth as venerable as it is free of exceptions. Wine and the vine go back hand in hand to the very portals of recorded history, and they are inseparable today. Go through the vineyards of California and the hospitable vineyardists will offer you wine, instead of water, to quench your thirst. When Noah left the ark, he turned immediately to viticulture:

" And Noah began to be an husbandman, and he

planted a vineyard; and he drank of the wine, and was drunken; and he was uncovered within his tent." [1] And on the other hand, even in the United States during prohibition, when our wine-growers have not been allowed to transform their vintage into wine for sale, wine grapes — as distinct from table grapes and raisin grapes — still constitute at least half of the crop. It is not without reason that the grape-grower is so often called a wine-grower, that the word " vintage " is used interchangeably to mean grape-gathering and wine-making, and that many of the most famous wines are called " growths."

The grape-vine — more properly, the genus *Vitis* — is widely distributed throughout the temperate parts of the world. It was thought by Linnæus to be indigenous to Persia, in the land south of the Caspian Sea. But this attractive theory was exploded by the discovery of wild indigenous vines in North America, and later in Mexico, China, Japan, India, and elsewhere. Its origin has become, like all ultimate questions, any man's guess, for the work of the archæologists and the palæobotanists has lately opened up new vistas into the past and in so doing has hopelessly confused the question: grape seeds have been found in the remains of prehistoric European lake-dwellings, and the evidence of fossils — leaves and seeds

---

[1] Genesis ix. 20–3. Learned commentators have pointed out that this lapse from sobriety was occasioned by his ignorance of the potentialities of his grapes on the new soil. In any case, his experience cannot be said to have done him much harm since he lived to the impressive age of 950 years.

— shows that wild species flourished in Germany, France, England, Iceland, Greenland, North America, and Japan during the Tertiary period and were forced southward during the succeeding ice age. The earliest of these fossil species resemble one of the wild American species (*V. cordifolia*) much more closely than they do the grapes of Persia. Let patriots take what comfort they can, in these days when wine is still frowned upon by the law, in the knowledge that America can claim with no little show of reason to be the birthplace of the vine.[1] They may derive some little additional satisfaction from the knowledge that of the thirty-two species of *Vitis* which are universally accepted, at least twenty are natives of America.

Yet, as a matter of fact, it is the single great European species which Linnæus named *Vitis vinifera*, the Old World grape, that gave wine to man — not merely the noblest of wines, but the bulk of all the wines that are made. Some thousands of varieties of this single great species exist today in the vineyards and botanical gardens of Europe, the fruit of many centuries of selection. There is evidence concerning the cultivation of the vine, and the making of wine, in Egypt between five and six thousand years ago, and the grapes were varieties of the species *vinifera*. The archæologists have shown beyond question that wine was dealt in as a commodity several thousand

[1] Professor E. W. Berry informs me that the very oldest fossil vines are those found in the upper cretaceous rocks of Colorado, New Mexico, and Alaska (estimated age, forty to fifty million years).

years before Christ in Mesopotamia, and the grapes were unquestionably *vinifera* varieties. There is a certain fitness in the recent re-establishment of wine-growing in Palestine, by the Jews, for when Moses led the Children of Israel out of Egypt, and after they had come within " walking-distance " of the Promised Land, he sent forth twelve men to reconnoitre, who " came unto the brook of Eshcol, and cut down from thence a branch with one cluster of grapes, and they bare it between two upon a staff." [1] The aroma of wine, as Butler declares, pervades the Bible from beginning to end — and, for that matter, the Talmud too. [2]

From the Promised Land the grapes of this species made their way, doubtless with the help of the Phœnicians, into northern Africa and eventually to Spain. The grape also made its way along the northern border of the Mediterranean, into Greece. It is needless to dwell on the place of honour which wine and the vine held in the successive civilizations of Greece. We even have some specific knowledge of their early wines. Homer tells us that they had grapes " purple and gold," which were " pressed out by the feet in the great vats." Hesiod liked nothing better, when the heat was greatest and the world ablaze, than to rest " under a shady ledge of rock with a bowl of Byblian

[1] Numbers xiii. 23–4. Many *vinifera* varieties — the Persian Sultanina, for instance — yield bunches of enormous size.

[2] Frank Hedges Butler: *Wine and the Wine Lands of the World.* New York, n.d. D. I. Macht: " References to Wine in the Talmud," *Science Monthly.*

wine." The Theophrastian account of the origin of wine, which is at least as credible and fully as interesting as the guesses of the scientists, is that the art of making wine was first imparted to the Greeks by Œnopœos, the son of Bacchus, and by them, more particularly the islanders of Chios, was imparted to other mortals. The Romans unquestionably derived their viticulture and their wine-making from Greece, although ancient Latium had its wild vines too. Œnotria, meaning "wine-land," was an early Greek name for southern Italy, later used for the whole of the peninsula, and Gibbon observes that " In the time of Homer, the vine grew wild in the island of Sicily . . . but it was not improved by the skill, nor did it afford a liquor grateful to the taste, of the savage inhabitants." Virgil makes reference to these wild vines in that remarkable text-book of viticulture, the Second Book of the *Georgics*. For many years the cultivated Romans would drink none but the famous Grecian wines, from Thasos, Rhodes, Cyprus, Melos, Ikaros, Andros, Naxos, Peparetos, and, above all, Chios and Lesbos, even as many Americans prefer to drink no wine at all if they cannot drink the bottled French and Rhenish wines — or at least wines bearing French or German labels. But in due time the Romans developed a complete array of wines of their own, from the unpretentious Sabine, which Galen prescribed as suitable for those between seven and fifteen, on through the light Galene, the Valiternian, the Signine, the Cæcuban, to the Massic, often mentioned by Horace, and the redoubtable Surren-

tine, which did not mature in much less than a generation. As Virgil [1] said:

> He who would number them, the same would wish
> To tell the tale of sand that Zephyr stirs
> On Lybya's waste, or when the East wind drives
> Most vehemently on the ships, to know
> How many rollers reach the Ionian strand.

It is impossible to go into Roman literature at any
point without bumping directly into wine. In time
the wines of Italy came to assume that place of honour
which was formerly enjoyed by those of Greece and
is now enjoyed (and strengthened by progressive, not
to say ruthless, publicity methods) by those of France.
Wine was the principal commodity in the shipping
of the Empire. Pliny could say, and Gibbon repeat,
"that of the fourscore most generous and celebrated
wines, more than two-thirds were produced from her
soil."

The viticulture of France did not stem directly, as
one might suppose, from that of Italy. A colony of
Ionian Greeks was established at Massalia (Marseilles)
in 600 B.C., and commenced the cultivation of the
vine. From Marseilles the vine quite naturally spread
up the Rhone valley. The first vines brought under
cultivation were the indigenous varieties, and these
were apparently followed by immigrant vines from
Greece. It is interesting and perhaps significant that
the most important grape of the Rhone valley today,

[1] *Georgics*, Book II. Translated by T. F. Royds. I do not vouch
for the quality of the translation, as poetry.

15]

the grape which gives their special quality to such wines as Hermitage and Châteauneuf-du-Pape, bears the name of Syrah. One of its still-current synonyms, Shiraz, reveals immediately its Persian origin, and it seems likely that its name escaped Romanization in this way. There is no doubt that this trans-Alpine wine-growing seriously worried the Romans, for in the time of Cicero there was a law of the Republic which forbade the cultivation of the vine beyond the Alps, an effort to stifle competition under the pretext of encouraging the growth of grain in those parts. The conquest of Gaul by Julius Cæsar (58–51 B.C.) proved also, however, to be a conquest of Gaul by the vine. During the second century the spread of the vine was unhindered,[1] and it was during this period that viticulture was introduced into the most northerly regions, along the left bank of the Rhine in Alsace, the Rhenish Palatinate, Rhenish Hessia, and the Moselle valley.

By the first quarter of the fifteenth century wine-growing had reached the Canary Islands and Madeira. And from that day to this the efforts to diffuse the culture of the grape — and especially of the *Vitis vinifera* — have been unceasing. Sometimes these efforts have been successful, more often not; but the work continues even today.

[1] The Pagus Arebrignus is believed, by M. d'Anville, to be the same as the district of Beaune, where some of the most famous Burgundies are grown.

3

During these many centuries the vine underwent much modification, and thousands of new varieties came into being. There are today varieties best suited to every type of European soil, others adapted to the heat of the Mediterranean basin and to the rigours of the Rhenish winter, others notable for their great productivity, and some, usually fitful and reluctant producers, which from the unique qualities of their wines are known as the noble plants. Among these noblest of vines are the Pinot Noir and its several sub-varieties, from which all true Burgundies are made; the Chardonnay, or White Pinot, which yields Chablis, Pouilly, and the other white Burgundies; the Riesling, which dominates the Rhine and Moselle districts; the Cabernet Franc and the Cabernet Sauvignon, which are the basic grapes of the finest vintage clarets; the Sauvignon Blanc and the Semillon, which are grown in the great Sauternes vineyards; the Sirah, of the Rhone valley; the Pedro Ximenes and Palomino, which are the characteristic sherry grapes. The coarser but more productive vines, from which the greater part of the world's wine is made, are no less famous, and their history, if less distinguished, is long and as honourable. Such are the Aramon, Alicante, Gamay, Carignane, Terret Noir, Kadarka, Grignolino. And in addition there is no considerable vine-growing region without its local pets, grapes little known the world over, but each possessing its special quality and yielding its unique wine.

No one can say when or how these varieties came into being. There are so many, and their qualities vary so widely, that some have supposed them to have resulted from the hybridization of several species. But those species, as Bioletti says, are now merely hypothetical, and all of these European varieties are now placed in the one species, *Vitis vinifera*. Many of them were unquestionably the seedling offspring of two different varieties of the species, planted near each other. Most of such seedlings, of course, disappeared without ever being recognized; now and again some particularly happy union might be discovered, and the new variety isolated and reproduced from one generation to another. For the vine may be propagated not only from seed, but also from cuttings taken from a vine in full vigour. The latter is the customary means of propagating. The vine grown from a cutting, unlike the seedling, is literally an offshoot of the parent, in which there can be no suspicion of an exotic strain. It is thanks to this asexual propagation that a great vine, once developed, becomes the permanent property of mankind; it is thanks to this that such varieties as the Sirah have continued absolutely unchanged through thousands of years; the vast Sirah vineyards of today are literally extensions of the first Sirah vine. New varieties have also appeared through mutation. The manner in which mutants — or biological sports — come into being is very little understood, but the vine gives rise to them much more frequently than do many other forms of life, and it may be that this is the greatest single factor in the development of the species' many varieties. Yet their very unexpectedness, their liability to appear at any time or not at all, or to die out without ever having been discovered, increases the difficulty of understanding these mutants.

The character of the vine, furthermore, is profoundly modified — more so than that of many other plants — by the nature of the soil and climate in which it grows. It is true that the modifications wrought by soil and climate are not permanent, and that, given its original environment, a vine will invariably reassume its original characters; yet the fact is that a variety grown, say, in the Médoc and in Algiers or southern California will show distinct differences in the quality of its fruit and its manner of growing.

The important point is that all these varieties developed without the conscious help of man, save as he found occasionally a valuable variation and perpetuated it. During the last half-century, thanks to the dramatic appearance of a succession of vine-diseases in Europe, which swept across its vineyards in epidemic fashion, the haphazard evolution of the vine has been replaced by conscious selection. The first of these plagues was the oidium, or powdery mildew, which attacks the fruit directly, reducing the yield of the vineyards, preventing perfect ripening, and imparting a peculiar and very special flavour to the wine.[1] There were two obvious methods of

[1] The French speak of such wines as *oïdiés*.

fighting the oidium. One was to replace the traditional varieties of vine with varieties whose fruit was not easily affected. The other was to cling to the traditional vines and to fight the disease itself by means of sprays and other forms of vineyard hygiene. Accordingly a search for immune varieties promptly began, and the French were soon importing and experimenting with certain of the native American varieties, which are markedly different in root, vine, and fruit characters from the European varieties. American vines have never yielded very good wine on European soil, and the Europeans were willing to tear out their traditional vines and plant the American substitutes only as a last resort. Luckily such drastic action proved unnecessary, for chemical means of combating the oidium were discovered. A start had been made, however, in the conscious selection of vines.

But the American vines, in turn, introduced into Europe another and much more dreadful plague, the phylloxera, a tiny plant-louse which attacks leaves and roots. The roots of the American vines are hard and firm and offer scant foothold for the louse. But the European vines have succulent roots, and the lice fell upon them with great relish: a couple of years of this feeding and the vine was dead. The pest was unwittingly introduced on the roots of American vines, and the sixties and seventies of the last century were years which the European vine-growers still recall with horror, for no way could be found to stop its relentless march. It was soon scattered through

Germany, Switzerland, Austria-Hungary, Italy, Russia, Turkey; but its worst ravages took place in France, where the natural conditions most favoured its spread. In 1875 the French production was 2,216,258,600 gallons; by 1879 it had dropped to 679,257,361 gallons. Unlike the oidium, the phylloxera cannot be fought by any prophylactic method; though the plant-pathologists have been grappling with the problem for more than half a century, no practical chemical or other method of checking its spread, save by flooding the vineyards periodically, has ever been found. Consequently the only defence was here to discover ways and means of immunizing the vine itself. M. Laliman, of Bordeaux, was the first man to observe and announce, in 1869, that the American roots were relatively resistant to the phylloxera, and his discovery was promptly confirmed by several American scientists. M. Gaston Bazille, of Hérault, attempted in the same year to put this resistance to practical use by grafting the traditional vines upon American roots. His experiments were successful.

Yet simple grafting was only a step toward solution, for it was quickly found that *all vinifera* varieties will not grow on *any* American root. And it was also discovered that some American species are much less resistant to the phylloxera than others. The problem was to develop new hybrids having specific characteristics and affinities. Thus the work of scientific, controlled selection by geneticists working, not on whim, but in accordance with the Mendelian laws of inheritance was made of the most immediate practical importance to vine-growers. The wine regions of Europe are today dotted with schools and co-operative or governmental viticultural and œnological stations where this work is being carried on. Thousands of varieties have been developed, most of them rejected, and some accepted. But the work is very slow, since a final conclusion as to the fitness of a given root-stock for a given scion cannot be reached in much less than twenty years. This work has also taken a good deal of the quaintness and naïveté out of wine-growing; it is characteristic that these root-stocks, unlike the old traditional grape varieties, have desperately business-like names, as, for instance, Mourvedre x Rupestris No. 1202, and Couderc plus Berlandieri x Riparia 33EM.

But though grafting on American roots has saved the vineyards of the old world and perhaps saved the species *Vitis vinifera* from eventual complete extinction, it is not wholly satisfactory. Grafting is expensive and laborious. Thus the geneticists have long been working on a parallel problem: that of developing what are called " direct producers " — that is, vines which do not require grafting, but, grown on their own roots, will yield fruit directly suitable for wine-making. " Thus," says Akenhead,[1] " geneticists now are seeking to localise in the leaves of direct producers the quality of resistance to mildew and to oidium, and in the roots that of resistance to phylloxera possessed by the American vines, while in the fruits the aim is

[1] *Viticultural Research*, by D. Akenhead, p. 15.

the fixation of the essential vinifera characteristics, the size of berry and the freshness of taste. Contrariwise an attempt is made to eliminate the inconvenient characteristics of both parents."

The work on direct producers has been less successful than that on the development of new rootstocks, and naturally so, for in the breeding of these many more factors have to be considered. The ability of vines to resist disease has been greatly improved, but so far the characteristics of the fruit have differed greatly from those of such distinguished vines as Pinot, Cabernet, and Semillon. The introduction of the new vines into regions famous for wines of certain types, as Hewitt says, " is not to be thought of." Yet there is no reason to suppose that in time these labours will not have their reward.

In the United States, where conditions are so different — and so much more important to the readers of this book — the development of new varieties has taken an entirely different course. For here the pioneers found no established varieties, but only wild species, and the history of American viticulture is largely that of the taming of these wild species. Before going into that story, which is set forth in some detail in the next two chapters, the principal wine regions of the world ought first to be reviewed.

4

Despite the spread of viticulture, Europe remains to this day the great wine-making region of the world.

So great is the prestige of its wines that all other wines, wherever produced, are inevitably called upon to stand the test of comparison with them. And of Europe, it is France pre-eminently that is the wine-making nation. More than half of all the wine produced in the world is made in France and in French North Africa, which, viticulturally, is really a part of France. Every department of France save two or three grows wines. But there are three regions in particular whose renown is so great and overwhelming that in any discussion of wines they overshadow all the rest. These are the valley of the Gironde (Bordeaux), Burgundy, and Champagne.

The port of Bordeaux, which is located some distance in from the mouth of the Gironde in south-western France, has been the centre of a great wine trade since the fourth century. It is famous not only for the fine wines grown in the district immediately surrounding it (the department of the Gironde) but for the lesser wines of the interior which are brought there for blending and shipment. The Bordeaux region yields an immense variety of wines, of every degree of excellence, but the most famous of all are the great classed growths of the Médoc, such as Château Latour, Château Lafite, Châteaux Margaux. It is from this region also that the white and red Graves come from, so named for the gravelly soil on which they are grown, of which the most famous is the red wine from Château Haut-Brion, and the white Sauternes, the most celebrated of which is Château

Yquem,[1] probably the most famous single growth in the world; also the white wines of Barsac, and the Côtes, Entre-deux-Mers, and Palus wines. The latter are the relatively inferior wines grown on the lands directly along the banks of the Gironde and the two streams which join to make it, the Dordogne and the Garonne. The characteristics of all these Bordeaux wines differ so greatly that it is impossible to find a common denominator for them. But of the red Médocs the most pronounced characteristics are their extreme fineness of bouquet and delicacy of body.

The rich and deeply coloured wines of Burgundy are, among red wines, second only to the wines of Bordeaux (and superior to them in the opinion of a great body of œnophiles: the battle between the partisans of the Bordelais and the champions of the Bourguignons never ends). As a wine-growing district Burgundy is very old, and a great mass of legend and tradition has grown up around it. The most renowned Burgundies are grown on the slopes of a chain of hills, about forty miles long, the Côte d'Or, which lies between Dijon and Chagny, in the eastern part of France. Along this slope are stretched the venerable vineyards of Chambertin, Clos-Vougeot, Romanée-Conti, Richebourg, Corton, Pommard, Volnay, and the others. Such is the prestige of the wines grown on this slope of gold that, it is said, generals have ordered their troops to present arms while marching

[1] One matter-of-fact fellow has written, of the vineyards of Yquem: " Each vine is cared for as carefully as the finest horse or cow would be."

25]

past the vineyards. The world of œnophiles is agreed that for sumptuousness of bouquet, and the substance to back it up, the Burgundies are unequalled. The white wines of this region, made from the White Pinot, or Chardonnay, such as Pouilly, Montrachet, Chablis, Meursault, if somewhat less famous, are fully as much appreciated by those who know them. The differences between the Burgundies and the Bordeaux extend even to the systems of cultivation and vinification. In the Bordeaux region the fine wines are the product of great estates, the châteaux which give to each growth its name, and it is possible to carry out the entire operation of wine-making, from the cultivation of the vine on through to the final bottling and packing, on the estate. The advantages of this system, in assuring the most scrupulous care in cultivation and in every step of the making and aging, are apparent; for each château is thus compelled to stand directly behind its own wine. But the vineyards of Burgundy are split into tiny holdings of an acre or two. There are some eighteen thousand wine-growers on the Côte d'Or, and fourteen thousand of them cultivate less than one hectare (two and one-half acres) apiece. The result is a dozen different Cortons, or Pommards, or Chambertins for any given year, since each proprietor is at liberty to dispose of his vintage as he wills — to make the wine himself, to sell his grapes under contract to one of the great Burgundy shippers, or to join in co-operative enterprise with his fellows. The co-operative scheme has been gaining popularity for some time among the individual proprietors; under this the *cuvage*, or vinification, is undertaken in common, so that the product from a given parish is uniform, and much of the former confusion, with consequent possibilities of fraud and misrepresentation, is eliminated. There are now a dozen or so co-operative wineries, making the *grands vins* from the Pinot grapes. This arrangement has worked very satisfactorily, both for the participants and for wine-drinkers, since the co-operatives exercise a care in vinification which is beyond the means and abilities of all save a few individual proprietors. Because of the fundamental difference, however, the wines of Burgundy are known as *cuvées*, or vattings, or marks, rather than *crus*, or growths, as in the region around Bordeaux.

Burgundy includes, in addition to the vineyards where fine wines are grown from the Pinot, a great many vineyards which are given over to coarser and more productive vines, the Gamay for red, the White Gamay and Aligoté for white. These yield wine that is in no way distinguished, but the yield is much greater. Unfortunately these Gamay wines are as much entitled to the appellation of " Burgundy " as the fine wines, a state of affairs which can be very misleading.

The districts to the north and south of it are frequently, and reasonably, grouped with the Côte d'Or proper. North and west is the region of Basse Bourgogne, from which the white Chablis comes; and to the south extends a series of less well-known *côtes* which are geographically identical with the Côte d'Or. These yield the wines of Chalon, Mâcon, Beaujolais, both red and white, which bear a family resemblance to the more famous Burgundies.

Champagne, the home of Dom Pérignon's sparkling wines, has already been discussed sufficiently for the purposes of this book. It suffices here to say that they easily maintain their prestige over all the other sparkling wines of the world, and also to say that the district produces many fine still wines as well, red and white.

These are the most famous wine regions of France. There are others, of the second order, which are less famous because they have not had the good fortune to be so greatly exploited, or because their wines do not travel well, or because the regions are not favourably situated as regards the channels of trade. Such are certain districts of the Loire valley, the Jura wines, those of the Garonne, and those of the valley of the Rhone, grown between Lyons and Marseilles.

But all of these " fine wine " regions yield only a fraction of the wines produced in France. For the bulk of the French wines — the wines on which the French really live — are the *vins ordinaires* produced in the Mediterranean departments which stretch from the Spanish border on the west to the Maritime Alps on the east. Of the whole French production of 50,000,000 hectolitres a year, these yield a good 27,000,000. And the greatest of these is Hérault, directly in the centre, where the astoundingly prolific Aramon [1] covers the land like a blanket. Here wine-making becomes a basic industry, being conducted in great co-operative wineries on a scale that is staggering. The largest of these, at Marsillargues, is equipped to handle as many as eight hundred tons of grapes a day. Of the wines grown in this region, de Cassagnac declares that " whatever their character, they are always distinguished by something excessive. If they are sweet, they are extremely so. If dry, their dryness verges on bitterness."

Across the Mediterranean, in Algeria, lies the other great source of the common French wines. There, again, wine-making is big business, conducted on a fantastic scale. The Algerian wines resemble those of the Midi, save that they are richer in alcohol and of better colour. They are by custom blended with French wines of complementary qualities.

Germany. Much of Germany lies in the latitudes where nature will not support the grape, or at least where seasons of sufficient warmth and sunshine are so rare that its cultivation is not practicable; yet it is a curious fact that most of the fine dry wines are grown at or near the limits of grape culture. So, though the production of German wines is very

[1] Guy Knowles, the British translator of de Cassagnac's *French Wines*, states in a note that " Aramon is an American stock. It is of a very vigorous habit of growth and thrives anywhere." The assumption of most Europeans that all American grapes are bad has led Mr. Knowles to the curious conclusion that since the Aramon is a grape of mediocre quality, it *must* be American. Actually, according to the ampelographic authorities, it is a variety of *Vitis vinifera*.

limited, and subject to many hazards, those which are produced are for the most part of fine quality. These wines have long been famous, especially in England, and the trade in them has existed as far back as the times of Edgar, Ethelred II, and Edward the Confessor.[1] Robert Greene, that " witty Bohemian of good intention but poor performance," is said to have died (in the time of Elizabeth) of a surfeit of pickled herrings and Rhenish wine. The growth is not specified. The most keenly appreciated of all are the wines grown in the Rheingau, a portion of the north bank of the Rhine, not more than fifteen miles long. Here are the famous vineyards of Rüdesheim, Schloss Johannisberg, Österreich, Geisenheim, and Rauenthal. The generic name for these wines, *hock*, is taken from the wines grown about the village of Hochheim, which were the first to achieve popularity abroad.

In Rhenish Hesse, on the opposite bank of the river, are grown other hocks, which are more plentiful, but are generally conceded to be inferior to those of the Rheingau. The wine known as *Liebfraumilch*, thanks partly to its rather audacious name, is the best known of these. In Rhenish Bavaria (the Palatinate) still larger quantities of wine, red as well as white, are grown. The qualities of these are quite distinct from those of the hocks. And in Franconia, in the central part of Bavaria around the town of Würzburg, are grown the *Stein* wines, very pale and with a subtle, flower-like bouquet, which come only in the *Bocks-*

[1] *In Vino Veritas*, by André Simon, p. 73.

beutel, or green flagon-like bottle — wines which the true *Feinschmecker* counts the peer of the best Rhenish wine.

The Moselles have always competed with the hocks for popularity among the German wines. These are the delicate and richly perfumed white wines, which are grown on the steep and slaty terraced slopes of the Moselle and its tributaries, the most northerly wine-growing region of the world. The name of Berncastel comes to mind immediately as that of the most famous of all the Moselles. These wines are grown largely from the Riesling grape, but they are paler than the hocks, and the peculiar Riesling bouquet, at once powerful and delicate, is in them especially pronounced. Much fake Moselle is made by the addition of elder-flowers to light white wines of ordinary quality. Although that part of the Moselle valley lying in Lorraine has now come under French sovereignty, the fact is that the best of the Moselles are still grown in the German part of the valley between Treves and Coblenz.

Italy. Only France produces more wine than Italy. And there are sound reasons why the wines of Italy should be more interesting to Americans than the wines of France. For in the United States wine-growing has always been much more in the hands of the Italians than the French, and it is our great Italo-American population which has always consumed the bulk of the American wines. And, finally, though the wine-makers of California have always sought to reproduce the more stylish wines of France, in order to snare the high-toned trade, the fact is that our California wines, if left to themselves, resemble much more closely the wines of Italy, particularly of northern Italy, than those of Bordeaux and Burgundy.

For many years, and despite the glorious reputation of Rome, the name of Italy was synonymous with slovenly viticulture and slipshod wine-making. Viticulture still followed the ancient Roman practice of training on trees, and the harvesting could not be done without the aid of the tallest ladders. Naturally much of the power of the vines went into the making of wood instead of fruit. But when the phylloxera struck Italy, it proved in one way a boon, for it provided an opportunity for the introduction of a more enlightened practice, as the vineyards were replanted. And for many years now the Italians have sought to make the most of their superb climatic endowment. The best of the Italian wines now compete, and properly, with the finest wines grown anywhere. There is an old Italian saying, quoted by Butler,[1] to the effect that " the Barolo, like the people of Piedmont, is strong and severe; the Chianti is pretty, delicate and lively, like the people of Tuscany; the Lacrima Christi is hot and fiery, like the Neapolitans; and the Marsala is strong and generous, like the Sicilians." That summary, like all such generalizations, is open to criticism in point of detail; yet it does sum up pretty accurately the qualities of the wines grown in the principal regions of Italy. The aristocratic vines of Italy are the Nebbiolo, whose wines closely re-

[1] *Wine and Wine Lands of the World*, p. 95.

semble the best red wines of Bordeaux; the Barbera, whose wines are big and deeply coloured and rich in tannin; the Refosco, which also gives wines resembling those of the Médoc; and the Freisa, whose strawberry-like bouquet yields highly characteristic wines. These, together with many of the less well-known Italian vines, have been planted in California.

Spain. To the world, Spain is the home of sherry. Actually, sherry constitutes but a part of the total wine-production of the country, and its production is confined to the province of Andalusia, in the region around Jerez de la Frontera. The making of sherry is a very special art; and this wine — the sack of Falstaff — is surrounded by a body of tradition and a literature so rich that anyone who seeks to pursue the subject can have no difficulty in doing so. But Spain makes many other wines, both red and white, which are consumed locally or shipped to such great blending centres as Bordeaux. Few of these ever emerge into the world under their own names. Many of the most popular California red-wine grapes, such as Alicante and Carignane, may be traced back to Spain.

Portugal. Like Spain, Portugal is known chiefly for its great specialty. Port is, if possible, even more English than sherry; and since George Saintsbury has written of port,[1] anything which might be said in this place would be the most futile sort of supererogation. It is perhaps not superfluous to add, however, one point which I do not recall that Professor Saintsbury set down. That is that port does not merit its

[1] In *Notes on a Cellar Book.*

reputation as the prime cause of gout. This is amply demonstrated by the fact that cases of gout are unheard of in Oporto.

In addition to its port, Portugal of course produces a great deal of dry wine, of which the red Collares and the white Bucellas, once much more popular than they are now (for there are fashions in wine), are highly esteemed by those who know them.

The Rest of Europe. As for the rest of Europe, it produces much wine, but little that calls for comment in this exceedingly superficial survey. Hungary, in particular, gives over a tremendous acreage to the cultivation of the vine. Its most famous wine is Tokay, made from the Furmint grape, which bears no resemblance whatever to the Tokay grape which may be bought in every American grocery-store. Tokay, actually, is not one wine, but a whole palette of wines, ranging from the celebrated Tokay *essence*, the consumption of which is confined largely to reigning houses, down through the whole scale of heavy sweetness to wines of comparative dryness and austerity. The dominating grapes of the less presuming wines of Hungary are the Kadarka for red wine and the Steinschiller for white. The German varieties are also grown a good deal. Other nations of central and southern Europe — Switzerland, Austria, the Balkans, and Greece — produce much wine, but little of it ever gets beyond the national frontiers. The wines of Russia, however, perhaps merit an extra word or two; for these wines are beginning to carry more weight in the world than they used to, and it may be that

[34

with the end of prohibition we shall have the pleasure of tasting them occasionally. The French, already hard pressed by the wines of Italy and the younger wine-growing regions, are already beginning to lament the possibilities of Bolshevik competition. The vine thrives in the peninsula of the Crimea, jutting out into the Black sea, and in Georgia and the Caucasus. Rhys Williams, in his very entertaining book of sketches of Russia, *The Russian Land*, describes a visit to the wine-growing region of Georgia, which lies at the eastern end of the Black sea:

" For wine runs in the Georgian's veins. Along with his mother's milk he gets his father's wine. Everywhere one sees fruits of the vine and the vine itself. Even over the façades of churches it climbs chiseled in stone, funny-faced lions blandly munching at the grapes. And the most sacred relic in Georgia, the cross the Virgin Mary placed in the hand of Saint Nina as she slept, is appropriately a grape-vine." He describes the meeting of a recently formed " cooperative ": " The big cool aromatic shed is crammed to the doors with all manner of men, ranging from ex-Prince Chavchavadze to his ex-lackey and the one-time village beggar. . . . At one end was a great trough, where last fall in shifts of day and night, knee-deep, they tramped out the grapes with their feet. . . . He pointed out the course of the juice piped from the big troughs into enormous jars set in the ground and tamped down with earth. . . . Everything goes according to program: the report on last year's gains, the fight against phylloxera by the grafting on of American roots, the donation of six hundred rubles for water-supply. . . . So the machine slips along smoothly until it comes to the election of three directors at salaries of one hundred fifty rubles a month. For these posts three Communists have been slated. But no sooner are their names read than, in a withering blast from the benches, breaks a hurricane of ' No! No! No! ' "

South Africa. The vine has been grown in South Africa since the middle of the seventeenth century, when it was introduced by the Dutch traders, whose object was apparently at first to cut themselves loose from their dependence upon French brandy. Under Governor Van der Stel wine-growing was encouraged, and the soil and climate proved congenial to the vines of Europe. In time wine-growing became one of the principal South African industries, and the South African wines, especially those of Constantia, enjoyed great popularity. But for a variety of reasons the singular popularity of Constantia has declined. Today the South African wines, of which there are many varieties and degrees of excellence, are sold principally in the British Empire. The Government is very careful, always, to see that it is a bottle of " Empire " wine that is cracked over the prow when a new cruiser is launched. The wines are produced in the south-western districts, the bulk wines chiefly in Paarl, Worcester, and Stellenbosch, and the finer light red wines on the Cape, where the Constantia district is situated. All of the better-known European varieties are grown on the Cape, but they have acquired their special South African names. Thus the Riesling has become Old Stein, the Sauvignon Blanc has become Stein, Semillon has become White Greengrape, etc.

Australia. The first vines went to Australia toward the end of the eighteenth century, with the early colonists, and were planted in New South Wales. From there they were taken into the southern States of Victoria and South Australia, where they do very well. But despite the best efforts of the Colonial Office and the Empire boosters (these wines, too, are cracked over the prows of battleships; it is a use to which many of them are well suited), the " Empire " wines of Australia have never been well received. They are, for the most part, coarse and crude, and they suffer too much from brisk Anglo-Saxon promotion methods. It is said, by the stubbornly imperialistic, that the finest wines of Australia compare favourably with those grown anywhere; it is also said that few of these ever leave Australia; so it is not easy for the person of sedentary disposition to verify these contentions.

South America. The European wine grapes were taken to South America by the Spanish missionaries, and a considerable area is under vines in Mexico, Peru, Bolivia, and Chile. The wines of Chile are esteemed the finest that are grown in South America. In Argentina, notably in the province of Mendoza, which lies at the foot of the towering Andes, wine-growing has been undertaken, especially since the war, on a vast scale, for Argentina is a wine-drinking country. This region is the South American counterpart of Algeria and the French Midi, and during the war much ordinary wine was shipped from there to France, where it was issued to the men in the trenches. Travellers who have tasted these wines pronounce them very good.

The Rest of the World. It will not do to pass over the wine-growing islands in silence. These are, principally, the islands of the Mediterranean, and those of the Atlantic, the Canaries, the Azores, and Madeira. And in Asia the cultivation of the grape has been revived in recent years. China many years ago grew much wine, but the industry died out. In India, especially in the valley of Kashmir, wine-growing has been introduced with moderate success. Curiously enough, though the *vinifera* varieties are cultivated, the ubiquitous phylloxera has reached even that isolated region, and the vines must be grafted onto American roots. Japan is the home of a number of wild species of grape, yet so far, despite many efforts to introduce the wine grapes of Europe, this archipelago has not produced any wines worth speaking of. The wild species, unlike those of America, are totally unfit for domestication.

Chapter Two

OUR VINOUS ENDOWMENT

THE UNITED STATES is the greatest natural grape-
growing region in the world. More than half of all
the known species of *Vitis* are natives of North
America; so, if natural endowment means anything,
the United States has to be considered a land of great
viticultural promise. And it has been so considered for
some nine centuries already. Lief the Lucky, son of
Eric the Red, on the evidence of a visit here about
A.D. 1000, named it Vinland because of the great pro-
fusion and luxuriant growth of the wild vines which
he saw upon landing; and as Wineland the Good it
is mentioned in the old Icelandic literature. Most of
the later explorers, though none went so far as Lief,
had very flattering things to say about our vines.
Hedrick [1] quotes Amadas and Barlow, who visited

---

[1] *The Grapes of New York*, by U. P. Hedrick, with the assistance
of four others. The title of this work is misleading; it is the classic
work, not on the grapes of New York alone, but on all our native
grapes. It has been referred to freely in the writing of this chapter.
A series of articles entitled " A History of Grape Growing in Eastern
United States," by F. E. Gladwin, which appeared in the *Rural New
Yorker* during 1931, has also proved very valuable. Hedrick is director

what is now Roanoke Island in 1584 and reported a land " so full of grapes as the very beating and surge of the sea overflowed them. . . . In all the world the like abundance is not to be found." Captain John Smith, writing in 1606, mentioned two different kinds of grapes: " Of vines great abundance in many parts that climbe the toppes of highest trees in some places, but these beare but few grapes. Except by the rivers and savage habitations, where they are not overshadowed from the sunne, they are covered with fruit, though never pruined nor manured. Of those hedge grapes we made neere twentie gallons of wine, which was like our French Brittish wine, but certainely they would prove good were they well manured. There is another sort of grape neere as great as a Cherry, this they (the Indians) call *Messamins*, they be fatte, and the juyce thicke. Neither doth the taste so well please when they are made in wine." These " Messamins " were undoubtedly the Muscadines, which grow wild throughout the south-eastern United States.

In July 1616 Lord Delaware, the first man formally to propose the establishment of wine-growing as an industry in America, wrote to the London Company: " In every boske and hedge, and not farr from our pallisade gates we have thousands of goodly vines running along and leaping to every tree, which yealds a plentiful grape in their kinde. Let me appeal, then,

---

of New York State's agricultural experimental work, and Gladwin is horticulturist in charge of the New York Vineyard Laboratory at Fredonia. Other references will be found in the bibliography.

to knowledge if these naturall vines were planted, dressed and ordered by skilfull vinearoons, whether we might not make a perfect grape and fruitful vintage in short time? "

Though it still seems obvious that much of the North American continent is admirably suited to the growing of grapes, it is still more obvious to the person who takes the trouble to examine the countryside that grape-growing holds no great place in the hearts and minds of our rural population. The vast potential vineyard which Amadas and Barlow were able to imagine, and which Lord Delaware, and later many others, took steps to bring into being, remains today still almost wholly potential. In this chapter I propose to set forth some of the reasons why the promise has never been fulfilled, as well as to outline what development *has* taken place.

When Lord Delaware sent his letter to the London Company, that corporation shortly obliged by sending over a group of experienced French vine-dressers, together with an assortment of vines and cuttings of the finest European varieties. The assumption was of course that where wild grapes were to be found in such abundance, the tame ones would flourish also. Thus the Virginia colony had apparently every prospect of success in wine-growing. Yet despite soil and climate that were apparently well suited to the purpose, and experienced workmen, and the finest vines available, and the testimony of the native grapes, the experiment was a failure. The failure was laid at the time to the inability of the Frenchmen to get along with the other colonists. They quickly fell to bickering, the colonists complaining that " the french-men transported into this country for the plantinge and dressinge of vynes and to instruct others in the same, have willinglie concealed the skill, and not only neglected to plant any vynes themselves, but have spoyled and ruinated that vyniard which was, with great cost, planted by the charge of the late company, and yet received all favour and encour-agement thereunto, which has dishartened all the inhabitants."

But the Virginians were not deterred by this fail-ure. They tried the expedient, always popular, if seldom successful, of solving their problems by pass-ing laws. One of these laws required that each house-holder plant ten cuttings, and that he learn the man-ner of caring for them. This seems to have yielded little wine. Then there was a massacre, which wiped out the remaining traces of the Frenchmen's enter-prise, both human and horticultural. Another short-lived law sought to encourage local wine-making by forbidding the importation of wines from Europe. Then in 1630 the colony, instead of providing legal penalties for failure to cultivate, reversed its policy and offered premiums for successful cultivation. Still no wine — or so little that no one bothered to re-mark upon it. In 1658 the colony offered a premium of ten thousand pounds of tobacco to anyone growing " two tunne of wine " on a colonial vineyard. Finally a few driblets of wine got back to England. Yet these wines seem to have been coldly received, and the effort, like all of its predecessors, met with no real success.

These consistently unsuccessful attempts to introduce the grapes of Europe to American soil were not confined to Virginia. Other efforts, quite as fruitless, were being made in every colony. In 1629, at the urging of the Governor, the growing of European grapes was tried in the Massachusetts colony, and Charles II himself arranged to have them planted in Rhode Island. The Huguenots had settled in the Carolinas, and it was inevitable that the European vine should accompany them, and that they should make repeated efforts to establish vine-growing. In Georgia a number of varieties were imported from Portugal by one Abraham de Lyon, with official encouragement; but if wine was produced on any considerable scale, there is now no testimony to the fact; and presently his vines fell ill and died, for no apparent reason. Sweden lies beyond the northern limit of successful grape-growing, and in order that Sweden might be independent of the wine-growing nations of Europe the Swedish Queen encouraged her colonists, who were established along the Delaware in what was known as New Sweden, to see what they might do in the way of wine-making. Many varieties were brought from France and Spain, but the experiment was no more successful than the others.

These efforts to establish the European grape succeeded one another with hardly a break for more than two centuries — efforts more remarkable for their persistence than for their good sense, since not one of them was successful. All sorts of reasons except the right one were put forward to explain the failures. The vine-dressers proved to be lazy, or were scalped, or ran away; a more attractive crop, like tobacco, lured the proprietor; or, as it often seems, the vine-growers merely lost interest. But the truth is that invariably " a sickness took hold of the vines," a sickness which the growers could not account for and which left them quite helpless. No one seemed to realize, save an occasional crank, that the European vine does not necessarily flourish where other vines will. And in eastern America it succumbed to a number of indigenous vine-diseases toward which the native vines were tolerant. Far and away the most deadly of these was the phylloxera. The devastation wrought by this louse when it was introduced unwittingly into the vineyards of Europe has already been mentioned. Unquestionably it was the insidious attack of the phylloxera, feeding with deadly effect upon the fleshy roots of the European plants, that foredoomed every one of these early efforts to failure. The American vines differ radically from those of Europe in that their roots, being hard, are more or less immune to the feeding of the louse; and if the early settlers had given less thought to the exotic vines and had paid more attention to the taming of the native species, the course of American viticulture might have been different. If they had, the United States might today be a wine- instead of a gin-drinking nation.

Yet it is inaccurate to say that the native grapes

were entirely neglected. Certain of these species, even in their wild state, are suitable for eating and wine-making: the fox-grape, or *V. labrusca,* which chokes the woods of New England, the Appalachians and the north central states; the chicken-grape, a common name which serves duty for several species, notably *V. æstivalis* and *V. riparia;* the strange Muscadine grapes of the South, which have a hundred local names. It is possible to make wines, of a sort, from these even when they are gathered from the woods. They were to some extent used by the colonists. We have already seen that Captain John Smith was not unaware of their possibilities; and Lord Delaware, though he wound up by sponsoring the abortive introduction of European varieties, first actually suggested the domestication of the native species. There are scattered records all through our colonial and early republican history of small individual experiments both in domesticating certain of the wild species and in making wine from them. The French who settled in Louisiana appear to have been most successful; so successful, in fact, that the French at home sought to discourage their efforts by devices which recall the efforts of the Romans to put the quietus on Gallic viticulture. They were apparently more successful in this than the Romans, for after a few years the Louisiana wine-makers ceased to be heard from. In the South along the Atlantic coast there grew up also a modest local trade in the wines of the Muscadines. But it is not hard to understand why these experiments were, relatively, so few and so tentative.

For our grapes are radically different from those of the Old World, not merely in the structure of their roots and vines, but in the qualities of the fruit. The wild American kinds contain much less sugar [1] and much more acid than the European, and they are so different in appearance, flavour, and smell that they invariably startle and dismay those who are familiar only with the bland and mild-mannered European sorts. One must learn to enjoy the sharp spiciness of the Muscadines, and the faint suggestion of polecat which lurks beneath; and this is true likewise of the " foxy " grapes. The aroma of these grapes, translated into wine, comes strange to the person bred on claret and Burgundy. The " foxiness " of our most plentiful species, *labrusca*, has in fact always been the great stumbling-block to American wine-making. Just why this special aroma — which is to be found working full blast in such common grapes as Concord and Niagara — should be " foxy " is one of those mysteries with which students of grapes and wine have been contending for years. William Bartram, writing many years ago, said that " the strong, rancid smell of its ripe fruit, very like the effluvia arising from the body of the fox, gave rise to the specific name of this vine, and not, as many have imagined, from its being the favourite food of the animal; for the fox (at least the

---

[1] They differ in many ways not perceptible to the layman. For example, in addition to the " grape sugar " which predominates in all grapes, some of them contain a percentage of sucrose. There is also the obvious difference that our grapes have " slip skins," whereas the skins of European grapes adhere to the pulp and may be eaten.

American species) seldom eats grapes or other fruit if he can get animal food." Yet to compare this aroma, which most native Americans greatly admire in eating grapes, to the " effluvia " of the fox is pretty far-fetched. In an effort to verify Bartram's contention I have been at some pains to sniff the " effluvia " of several kinds of fox, in a number of celebrated zoos, and have been unable to detect the faintest resemblance. To call it " horsy " would be no more inaccurate and unsatisfactory.[1] The lack of a satisfactory word for this aroma illustrates most poignantly the difficulty which writers have always had when called upon to discuss odours and flavours. The English language badly needs improvement in the departments of olfaction and gustation. In the meantime, let us content ourselves as best we can with " foxy."

2

The great difference between the wines made from these native grapes and the conventional characters of European wines was probably the principal obstacle to their domestication. The first real impetus to the domestication of the native grapes was accidental. A Swiss named John Dufour organized, toward the end of the eighteenth century, the Kentucky Vineyard Society, to grow European grapes on a large tract in Kentucky, one of the few settled or partly settled regions where these grapes had not yet been tried and found wanting. His enterprise failed, like all of its predecessors, after the production of a trifling quan-

[1] Virgil speaks of an " ox-grape."

tity of wine. His vines were seized with the inexplicable " sickness," all except one variety, a black grape, which thrived. This grape he had secured from one Peter Legaux, a Frenchman who had tried his hand at viticulture (without success, of course) near Philadelphia and who supposed it to be a variety which had been imported as seed from the *vinifera* vineyards of the Cape of Good Hope. It was known by the names of Alexander or Cape, and later by many other names, such as Vevay, Clifton's Constantia, Schuylkill Muscadel, etc. The news of this grape spread rapidly. Dufour removed from Kentucky to Indiana and once more planted the varieties of *vinifera;* again the only one to survive was the Alexander. On the strength of this double success, the Alexander was widely planted, and nearly everywhere it throve. But before long certain iconoclasts were suggesting that it was not a European variety at all, but a bastard American which had fallen accidentally among its high-born cousins. Dufour denied this hotly and fought with all the savagery of an aroused pomologist to " save its character "; for it was Dufour's firmly held opinion that there could be no insult more dreadful than to call a grape an American. He died fighting, convinced to the end that he had established the European grape on American soil. Subsequent examination has shown the Alexander to contain, beyond all doubt, a predominance of native blood; it may well have been a chance hybrid of wild *labrusca* with one of Legaux's pure *vinifera* kinds. The Alexander is only a piece of pomological history now, for better kinds have displaced it.

But it served its purpose: it made the native grape respectable.

Thanks to the Alexander, the direction of American viticulture was turned toward the native vines. Prince, the author of the first genuine treatise on American vine culture, concluded, after a lifetime of investigation into the peculiarities of the vine, that the only sensible course was to cultivate the native species. John Adlum, writing in 1809, remarked in connection with the Alexander: " I think it would be well to push the culture of that grape without losing time and efforts in search of foreign vines." But in one sense this change came too late. Nearly two hundred years had been frittered away in fruitless, if well-meant, experiment; and during that time the opportunity to make of the American nation a wine-drinking people had been lost — perhaps for ever. Most Americans had long since ceased to regard wine-drinking as anything but a luxury, a form of conspicuous waste, and had come to prefer liquors, such as the whiskies distilled from our various grains, and the rum which could be made so cheaply from West Indian sugar-cane. It may be doubted whether the average farmer — who in Europe is a consistent wine-drinker — gave a thought to wine from year-end to year-end. Lacking whisky or rum, he always had his cider.

The success of the Alexander was followed quite soon by the appearance of two other native varieties, the Isabella and the Catawba. The Isabella need not deter us long, for its cultivation, though important for a time, has died out. It is of unknown origin, was introduced around 1816, and gained considerable popularity because of the fact that it ripened somewhat earlier than the Alexander and consequently could be grown in colder latitudes. In character it was not unlike the Concord.

The appearance of the Catawba was a much more important occurrence, and for years this variety was the principal cultivated American grape. Its actual origin, like that of the Alexander and the Isabella, is a mystery. Hedrick says that it made its debut in 1823, in the garden of John Adlum, in the District of Columbia; and Major Adlum said that he secured the cuttings from a Mrs. Scholl, of Montgomery County, Maryland. The Scholls had always called this grape Catawba; but Mrs. Scholl's father, to the great loss of science, died before he could be pinned down as to where he got it. The late T. V. Munson, one of our greatest viticulturists, said that it was found wild in the woods near the Catawba River, North Carolina, in 1801, but he gives no evidence to support his statement. There is also considerable mystery about the Catawba's botanical pedigree. Gladwin, the latest to write of its history, says: " Most agree that it is a derivation from the pure native *labrusca*." Others have contended that it is a hybrid, and the outspoken Munson wrote that it contains some *vinifera* blood, perhaps transmitted to some wild vine from one of the abortive vineyards of European cuttings. But all this may safely be left to the genealogically minded; the point is that it yielded a native wine which was the first to

[50

receive really serious and respectful attention.[1] Major Adlum wrote, apropos of his bringing this grape under the public eye: " In bringing this grape into public notice, I have rendered my country a greater service than I could have done had I paid off the national debt." And so he did. The original Nicholas Longworth, a man of immense labours on behalf of his country, whose passion for the vine was only equalled by his ability to inspire a like passion in others, planted it in his vineyards near Cincinnati in 1825; in return the Catawba established the everlasting fame, and more perdurable fortune, of the house of Longworth. Its wines, both still and sparkling, were much admired, and its culture spread very rapidly. The Catawba wines held their popularity right up to the establishment of prohibition. Shand mentions having run across a number of lots of sparkling Catawba at a British wine auction several years ago, and his subsequent wish that he might have tasted a bottle, " as a toast of requiescat to the ghosts of departed American vineyards."

Within a decade of the introduction of the Catawba — that is, by 1830 — grape culture had become a modest but commercially profitable industry. The Catawba was planted even more extensively in North

---

[1] I have successfully resisted the impulse, which has overpowered practically every writer on American grapes, to quote Longfellow's dreadful poem about Catawba wine, the one which goes:

> Very good in its way is the Verzenay
> Or the Sillery, soft and creamy,
> But Catawba wine has a taste more divine,
> More dulcet, delicious and dreamy. . . .

51]

Carolina than in Ohio, for an unfortunate characteristic of the Catawba is its slowness to ripen, and in the North it is frequently nipped by an early frost. Several other varieties had also been introduced and had achieved a certain popularity. In Virginia and the Carolinas a seedling of the wild *V. æstivalis* — a species from which several of our most important wine grapes have come — known as Norton's Seedling, was being cultivated to a slight extent. But, strangely enough, though this is still deemed the best of all our native red-wine grapes, it was not highly esteemed until at least a quarter of a century after its appearance, and then achieved its greatest popularity not in the region where it was originated, but in Missouri. In the South also the Muscadines, which constitute a family that is quite distinct from all other native species, had a good deal of local popularity. These grapes grow on vines which assume huge proportions, spreading sometimes over many thousands of square feet and supported by trunks many feet in diameter. There are white and black varieties of the Muscadines. The berries do not grow in bunches, but in small clusters of four or five berries; they are very large, possess thick leathery skins, and are soft and mushy within. Their powerful scent has already been alluded to. The best of the dark kinds are James and Flowers, but most popular of all is the bronzy green Scuppernong. There are many " original " Scuppernong vines. One of these stands on Roanoke Island; another, thought to have been found by a member of Sir Walter Raleigh's colony in 1554, was still standing on an island in the Scuppernong River, North Carolina, a few years ago. It was originally supported by a tree, which died and rotted away, leaving the vine to stand on its own huge trunk. In the North, wherever the Catawba could not be relied upon to come to maturity regularly, the Isabella was largely grown. But whatever else the virtues of this grape, they did not include the qualities sought by the wine-maker. The Clinton, a cultivated variety of *V. riparia*, and the parent of many admirable red-wine grapes, was making way slowly. All of the *riparia* grapes are small and unprepossessing in appearance, sour to the taste (although they contain sufficient sugar for wine-making, their sweetness is drowned out by an excess of acid), thick-skinned, and full of seeds; and their wine, thanks to the abundance of acid, is green and harsh when young. Yet an abundant acidity has its uses in wine-making, as we shall see later; and the Clinton has always been a useful fruit.

Grape-growing steadily expanded during the following two decades, so that by 1850 there were prosperous vineyards in the Ohio River valley, in central New Jersey, in the Hudson River valley, along the south shore of Lake Erie around Cleveland, in certain parts of the Carolinas, and in a part of Missouri around the town of Hermann. This district later earned considerable renown for a whole series of wine grapes, developed from species indigenous to that region, of which the most famous was perhaps the Missouri Riesling, a white-wine grape. The Chautauqua and Finger Lake districts of New York State — the latter of which has always yielded our best sparkling wines — were already giving signs of glory to come. Deacon Elijah Fay had established vineyards in the first of these, and the Reverend William Bostwick was the pioneering grower in the latter, thus maintaining in unbroken continuity the traditional affiliation between Church and vine.[1]

3

Then in 1852 occurred a great pivotal event in the history of American grape culture: the Concord appeared on the scene. Its introduction was important mainly because it turned the attention of grape-growers away from wine and toward the table. This grape was a pure seedling of the wild fox-grape, or *labrusca*, without trace of the blood of any other species. The fated seed from which the Concord was to spring was planted in 1843 by one Ephraim Bull, of Concord, Massachusetts. The vine came to bearing several years later, and was exhibited before the Massachusetts Horticultural Society in the year 1852. The person who is unacquainted with the hair-trigger passions and transcendent enthusiasms of the viticulturist simply cannot imagine the furor which it caused. Here are the reasons for the Concord's immediate and overwhelming

---

[1] Deacon Fay was a Methodist; the Reverend Mr. Bostwick was an Episcopalian. Let us admit, though, that the Protestant denominations have frequently strained this close affiliation, some of them even going so far as to serve unfermented bottled grape juice, and that with some misgiving, in sanitary paper cups, in the course of their communion services. It is the Catholic Church which has maintained an unwavering affiliation.

success: it produces so cheaply and abundantly that it makes a dismal joke of all competition; it is virtually indifferent to climate, growing rankly in both hot and cold regions, and flourishes in practically any soil; it is immune to most of the vine-diseases and thrives under neglect; it travels well and withstands storage moderately well; it does not winter-kill, which is to say, with the poet, that it successfully endures

> . . . the bitter change
> of fierce extremes . . .

and, finally, the fruit is good to look at, suitable for jam, and agreeable to eat " out of hand." [1] But it is not a satisfactory wine grape. Its strongly foxy aroma has just about as much subtlety as a one-reel movie comedy, and its sugar-content is ordinarily so low that a reasonably stable wine cannot be made from it without the addition of large quantities of grocery-store sugar. It is unfair to say that wine cannot be made of it at all, for much wine has been made of it (including, even, a " Concord Port "!), but these wines are so inferior to those which may be made from other native varieties that its overwhelming popularity among our

[1] But not, by any means, of the first quality. It is a truism among growers and merchants that people almost invariably buy fruits and vegetables on the strength of their appearance only, quite forgetting the presumably more important question of their quality as food. Munson says of the Concord: " The Concord being considered by the majority of persons, in regions where it is grown, as the standard market grape, it is used as the minimum standard of comparison for quality. . . . Nothing poorer than Concord should be tolerated. . . ."

growers has been the severest blow to the reputation of native wines that we have had to withstand. When presently the Concord proved also to be ideal for making bottled unfermented grape juice, its success turned into a riot. A monument stands at the site of the original vine — the original vine still flourishes today: one must add longevity to the Concord's other characteristics — but the wine-maker will worship at that shrine with mingled emotions. Today nine-tenths of all the native grapes grown are Concords; it so dominates the market that those who have not looked into the question are unaware that any other native blue or black grape exists.

But the Concord, to give it grudging credit, was important in another way. At the time of its exhibition Mr. Bull thought it to be a hybrid, a cross between the wild fox-grape and the Catawba. It is now denied that Concord is anything but a pure seedling of the wild vine; but the possibilities of developing new types by crossing were nevertheless well advertised. In the two decades which followed, American fruit-growers in every part of the country, amateur and professional, went hybrid-mad. New varieties, from parents crossed at random, were produced and exhibited by the hundreds. Most of these were worthless, the unhappy offspring of woefully unsuitable marriages, but the period also yielded several varieties which are still in the front rank of our native wine grapes. Attempts to cross the European *vinifera* varieties with the native grapes were particularly interesting, although most of the resulting hybrids were also failures, in which the worst characteristics of the European *vines* and the worst characteristics of the American *fruit* were hideously mingled. But among the second- and third-generation hybrids (those containing one-fourth *vinifera* blood or less) there were some which have turned out to be glorious successes. The greatest of these was (and is) the Delaware, which was named after Delaware, Ohio, the town where it first came into notice, and not after the Lord Delaware to whom we have already made obeisance, nor yet after the State of that name. It is difficult to resist growing lyrical over this lovely fruit. It is small and delicately formed, pale rose in colour, with a bloom of greyish lavender, and it grows in bunches that are plump and voluptuous: it is the finest of all our white-wine grapes, by general agreement. Chemically, according to Alwood, its wines resemble the richest wines of the German Palatinate; but we need not carry the comparison beyond the confines of chemistry, for that would be misleading. Although the Delaware was the finest, it was by no means the only good grape to make its appearance during that prolific period. Two hybridizers in particular, E. S. Rogers, of Salem, Massachusetts, and Jacob Moore, of Brighton, New York, were successful, horticulturally if not financially.[1] Rogers was fascinated by the possibilities of

---

[1] Most originators of fruits have died poor, thanks (1) to the absorbing nature of this art, which renders the practitioner more or less heedless of material reward; and (2) to the fact that the originator of a new plant had no protection under the law anyway, as had the inventor of a new type of clothes-pin or monkey wrench, until

improving our wild vines by marrying them with *vinifera*, and from a life of experiment he gave to the world some forty varieties, which are known collectively as Rogers's Seedlings. Most of these have some defect which has kept them from general cultivation, and in general his results may be said to have been more curious and interesting than practically valuable. His failure to affect the course of viticulture more directly was owing partly to the perverse delight which he took in testing his ability by bringing forth acceptable children from the most unpromising combinations of parents. Yet he is a great figure in American viticulture. Moore gave better grapes to the world than Rogers, and also died poorer. His two best were probably Brighton, a remarkable red grape whose wine was used a great deal formerly in the blending of New York State " champagne," and Diamond, a green grape which has always been in demand for both still and sparkling wines.

During this period also the American grapes made their famous expedition of mercy to France. Something has been said in the preceding chapter of the two great plagues, oidium and phylloxera, which swept over the vineyards of Europe during the nineteenth century. The oidium was first observed in 1845, and it seems likely that this, like the phylloxera, came in on American vines, for it is an indigenous American disease, and it is known that cuttings of Catawba and Isabella went to France as early as 1825, for purposes

the Patent Law was finally amended, in 1930, to take care of this anomaly.

of examination and study. At any rate, the disease got there, whether on those cuttings or in some other way. And, having arrived, it was followed by the importation of American vines. Between 1858 and 1863 a considerable number of varieties were sent over, and these in turn took over the phylloxera.[1] When the true seriousness of the phylloxera plague was realized, the demand for the American vines became very great, for the efficacy of grafting had not yet been discovered, and the French proposed to use these American varieties as " direct producers " to displace their own varieties entirely. The principal direct producers which the French tried were the Noah, for white wine, which resisted well both the phylloxera and oidium; Jacquez, a variety from *V. Bourquiniana*, known sometimes as the *southern æstivalis*, which is still grown for red wine in some parts of France; Clinton, for red wine; and Othello, which is a hybrid of Clinton and a *vinifera* variety. All of these resisted the oidium and the phylloxera, and the red wines were rich in colour and of sufficient alcohol and acidity. But they all had traces of the foxy aroma which the French profess so to abhor in American grapes, and the calcareous soils of Europe appear to bring out this aroma to an excessive degree. When the possibilities of grafting were discovered, these direct producers were for the most part abandoned, or cut to the roots and used as grafting stocks *in situ*, and the French were thus enabled to return to their traditional vari-

[1] The French say that the phylloxera is an indirect consequence of Columbus's discovery of America.

eties. The demand from then on was for American roots only. As a matter of fact, the more stubborn and conservative French growers for long were suspicious not only of the American direct producers, but of the whole art and science of grafting, and the argument between the opponents and the proponents of grafting raged well into the twentieth century. The contention of the die-hards was that the root-stocks materially alter the character of the scion in both vine and fruit, to its detriment, shortening the life-span of the vine, increasing its susceptibility to physiological troubles, and adversely affecting the quality of the wine. One still reads elaborate discussions of the relative merits of pre-phylloxera and post-phylloxera wines, arguments which can well run on for ever, since pre-phylloxera wines are now practically unobtainable. But as a matter of fact, in 1898 elaborate experiments were made at Corton, in the Burgundy region, where wines were prepared from Pinot grafted on Riparia, and Pinot growing on its own bottom (in elaborately disinfected soil), and the results were actually favourable to the wines from grafted vines; such experiments have been repeated elsewhere, many times over, usually with similar conclusions. The last great offensive of the die-hard brigade was in 1908, when Professor L. Daniel, its French generalissimo, issued a withering and unequivocal denunciation of the whole grafting business, flatly advocating the disinfection of the soil, at whatever expense, rather than a continuance of what he genuinely believed to be a suicidal practice. It is as academic now to revive that controversy as it is to argue over the relative virtues of protection and free trade, or to lay plans for altering the course of the Gulf Stream; grafting on American roots is practised now in every *vinifera*-growing region of the world, and is apparently here to stay.

But the European relief work was only incidental to American viticulture, which continued slowly and steadily to expand. The notion of growing European vines in the eastern United States had been abandoned by practically everyone — though it is a perpetually tempting notion, and there has probably never been an enthusiastic student of grape-growing who has not, at one time or another, turned to it more or less wistfully, unwilling to believe until he has the testimony of his own eyes that he is pursuing a mirage. One finds even today that the growing of them, on grafted roots, of course, is being tried at so severely practical an institution as the New York State Vineyard Laboratory at Fredonia. But those few who still hoped to do it on a commercial scale were given their last blow around 1880, when California viticulture began to compete with that of the East. In California, where conditions of soil and climate differ radically from those of the East, the European wine varieties thrive,[1] and that remarkable State is capable of producing fair imitations of most of the principal types of European wine. By 1880 the shipments of California wines to the East had reached such proportions as seriously to menace the Eastern wine-making industry, and before long California was growing about eighty-five

[1] California viticulture is fully discussed in the next chapter.

per cent of all the grapes grown in this country, for whatever purpose, a proportion which it has continued to maintain with only slight fluctuations.

4

Although the field of Eastern wine-growing was thus sharply delimited, Eastern wine-making was by no means doomed; and as a matter of fact the cultivation of our native grapes has never ceased to increase, though the increase has naturally been at a more moderate rate since California came into its own. By the turn of the century there were several hundred thousand acres devoted to our native varieties. The great Chautauqua and Finger Lake districts of New York had continued to increase their acreage, and the Niagara peninsula district had been added. The region around Cincinnati, where Nicholas Longworth and his Catawba had joined in happy co-operation, had declined, but the northern part of Ohio along Lake Erie had heavy acreage, and the superior virtues for wine-growing of the Lake Erie islands, especially Kelley's Island, were being exploited. Large bodies of water exercise a desirable influence on climate from the standpoint of the vine-grower. They delay the budding of the vines in the spring until the period of sudden frosts is passed, and in the fall they reduce the likelihood of frost during the season of ripening. In addition there were considerable districts in Pennsylvania, Michigan, Illinois, Indiana, Kansas, Missouri, Arkansas (the Ozarks), Oklahoma, Georgia, the Carolinas, and Virginia. The central part of New

Jersey, around Egg Harbor, was also producing good wines.

The reason why these districts were not utterly blotted out by the competition of California is fairly obvious. The wines from native grapes are unique. The wines of California, being grown from the grapes of Europe, inevitably bear a certain resemblance to those of Europe, in spite of the modifications imposed by differences in soil and climate. And since most wine-drinkers have been taught to prefer the European models, it is inevitable that they should dominate the markets. Furthermore, since the California vines are more prolific than most of our native species, California can in the long run, working on a large scale, grow grapes more cheaply. But in bouquet, flavour, body, and every other characteristic our native wines differ from those of Europe and of California — differ definitely and aggressively. Ordinarily this sharp departure from the traditional types has been looked upon as a sign of inferiority — as though there were some norm of excellence for wine which has been fixed for all time — and much time and effort has been wasted in the past in seeking, by blending or by manipulations during the making, to conceal the specifically American qualities of American wines. Yet an ardent minority has long insisted on the virtues of the native wines. And even the French [1] have admitted on occasion that their preference for the wines of France is to some little extent merely a matter of personal taste fashioned out of habit. We find such

[1] Well, a few of them.

sober authorities as Faes, Tonduz, and Piguet join-
ing to acknowledge that "the wines obtained from
[American] hybrids appear, on the whole, to be new
products, essentially differing as regards their characteristic qualities of bouquet and flavour, from the
wines produced from French vines to which the public has so long been accustomed." In a word, hardly
comparable at all: two Burgundies may be compared,
or a true *vin de Bourgogne* and a "Burgundy type"
from California; but not a Burgundy and an American Norton. The American wines not only are capable of, but cannot avoid, standing on their unique
qualities. It is these wines from our Eastern vineyards,
not those from the vineyards of California, that are
our truly characteristic wines, our wines of the country. And every wine-lover who is also a patriot must
find profound satisfaction in the knowledge that we
have certain wines whose unique and charming qualities cannot be duplicated anywhere else on earth, and
must hope earnestly for their constant improvement
and their wider recognition.

Yet there are many obstacles to the attainment of
that goal. The competition of California for the bulk
of the wine trade has already been mentioned. There
is also the fact that for eighty years the native grape-
growers have had their eyes turned away from the
production of wine grapes and toward the growing of
grapes for the table and for the so-called temperance
grape juice. Table grapes, in which appearance and
keeping qualities are the prime requirements, seldom
make good wine grapes. And as for the baneful influ-

ence of grape juice — what can one say? A good grape-juice grape must be everything that a wine grape is not. It must be low in sugar, or the grape juice will be cloying; it must also have a very pronounced flavour and smell before fermentation (most wine grapes have little odour; the bouquet develops after fermentation). The Concord fills these specifications admirably, and since it is also a popular table grape, and fine for grape jelly, the cuttings of Mr. Bull's original Concord vine now furnish nine-tenths of all the native grapes grown. Of the remaining ten per cent, the larger proportion of those vineyards are given over to our second most popular grape, the green Niagara, which is also an inferior wine grape.

Another handicap has been the comparative dearth of good work in œnological science, especially as it relates to the fitness of our native varieties for wine-making. William B. Alwood, an œnological chemist in the service of the Department of Agriculture, published during the early years of this century a series of papers which stand practically alone as competent studies of the specific problems of the growers and makers of native wines. His work was stopped by an ungrateful people. Practically the whole of the wine literature which had been built up before that demonstration of ingratitude relates to the wines of California. Hand in hand with this dearth of scientific work goes the apparent lack of interest among our pomologists, who are the men to whom we must look for the improvement of established varieties and the development of new. Munson, an estimable man, made many thousands of hybrids. But he confessed to a personal weakness for unfermented grape juice, and the task to which he dedicated his life was that of working out a series of table-grape varieties which, grown commercially, would supply our tables with grapes, blue, red, and white, continuously from early summer to late in the fall. A laudable enterprise, surely; but not of much interest to the wine-maker, who wouldn't make wine in the heat of summer if he could. Hedrick, the distinguished author of *The Grapes of New York*, is a systematic pomologist and as much interested in the pear, the plum, the apple, and the cherry; and the New York Vineyard Laboratory, under the capable direction of F. E. Gladwin, has done much more for table grapes than for wine grapes. Our experimenters have produced fifty table-grape varieties for every one having large possibilities for wine.

And finally the cause of native wines has suffered tremendously as the result of prohibition. Thanks to the scarcity of information about wine-making, the domestic wine-makers of the prohibition era have had no means of knowing what the good native varieties are and where they may be found. In their ignorance, they have been content to accept the Concord — or else they have tried the Concord and as a result given up wine-making entirely. There are many excellent native wine grapes, but how many know where they are grown? The Delaware is grown a good deal still in central New York (thanks to the fact that there is a certain demand for it for eating), and the Catawba is fairly common, but what of Iona, Dutchess, Diamond, and Elvira, from which so many of our best white still and sparkling wines were formerly made? Norton is grown a little here and there, in Missouri, on the Lake Erie islands. But what of those once popular varieties, Ives, Bacchus, Clinton, Cynthiana, from which so much good red wine used to be made? And what of Rommel and Missouri Riesling, and of Diana, America, Herbemont, Lenoir? It is a mistake to say that they are gone, for enlightened nurserymen still stock them, and occasional vineyards of them are scattered about the land; only their cultivation has sadly diminished, and some would be threatened with extinction were it not for the stubborn amateur and the occasional enthusiast among vineyardists.

With the spreading of information about these grapes, it may be that a demand for them will revive. And it is certain that with the ending of prohibition the demands of the professional wine-makers will bring them once again out of their obscurity. And it may be, when that time comes, that an intelligent interest in developing still better varieties may spring up. Such work is slow. Munson admitted that out of the 75,000 seedlings which he grew, not more than 100 could be looked upon as worth perpetuating; and time and the opinion of his successors have reduced that hundred already to a mere dozen at the outside. Yet it took many centuries for Europe to develop its thousands of varieties from a single species. When one reflects upon that fact, it seems altogether reasonable to suppose that we have no more than begun to explore the possibilities inherent in our twenty-odd species, or even of the half-dozen most promising of these. Our land, as Lief the Lucky observed three thousand years ago, is still a land of great viticultural promise.

Chapter Three

CONCERNING CALIFORNIA

In the year 1889 a prominent grocer of San Francisco was offering a list of some thirty wines, all of them bearing distinguished names. Among the clarets were such interesting growths as Margaux, Lafite, Pontet Canet, Mouton Rothschild, Pichon Longueville; among the Burgundies, Romanée Conti and Le Clos Vougeot. For white wines he had a number of Sauternes, including Château Yquem 1874, an important Rhenish growth, and several other things. As a contemporary writer [1] observed, this list did not include a single local wine. There was nothing on it to show that San Francisco lay at the very centre of California's best wine-growing region. In any self-respecting wine-growing region every dealer has the local wines

---

[1] *Wines and Vines of California: A Study in the Ethics of Wine-Drinking*, by Eunice Waite. San Francisco, 1890. It has frequently been remarked that women cannot be true wine-lovers. A reading of Miss Waite's useful if perhaps over-enthusiastic book should dispel that notion. Another wine book by a woman is *Bouquet*, by G. B. Stern, the novelist, which is the delightful record of a wine-drinking tour of France.

at the top of the list, in large letters. He does not wish, nor would he dare, to do otherwise.

But the service of this grocer to San Francisco's œnophiles did not stop with providing this imposing selection of European names: his prices were equally interesting. He wanted only twenty-five dollars a case for his Vougeot and a mere fifty-four dollars for his Romanée Conti, a wine which in France, leaving out the long and expensive voyage to California, in a good year is worth its weight in silver if not in gold. It is not usually considered a grocer's wine.

The truth is, of course, that these wines were not at all what they purported to be. The chances are that every one of the grocer's wines was produced within a radius of three hundred miles of the grocery store — only the wine-makers had sold their birthright for a mess of fancy foreign labels.

This ability to reproduce the wines of Europe is at once the greatest blessing and the greatest misfortune of vine-growing California. It is only in California that the Old World grape, the species *Vitis vinifera*, can be grown successfully. So, unlike the grape-growing regions east of the Rockies, where, as we have seen, domesticated varieties of the native species are exclusively cultivated, California's vineyards have always been devoted to the growing of the European varieties.

Furthermore, it is not merely the wines of some one part of Europe that California may reproduce, but the wines of practically every part of that wine-growing continent. For California is a very large State, and

within its boundaries are to be found a great many different soils and every variety of climate. The vineyards of Europe all lie within fourteen degrees of
latitude; California extends over ten degrees. Thus
practically every part of wine-growing Europe, from
the northern-most vineyards of the Moselle to the
hot alluvial plains of the Midi, finds its counterpart
there.

The Coast counties by common consent yield California's best dry wines, red and white. These fifteen
counties have San Francisco Bay as their hub and
stretch out to the north and south of it. In general the
rule is that those counties running directly into the
bay produce the finest wines. The three exceptions to
this rule are Marin County, which forms the north
side of the Golden Gate, and San Francisco and San
Mateo counties, which lie to the south of it. These
are troubled a good deal by fogs and chill. These
hinder ripening and increase the susceptibility of the
vines to disease. The very finest of the wines have
always come from the vineyards of Sonoma, Napa,
and Alameda counties (the Livermore Valley of the
latter), with Santa Clara and San Benito counties
pushing them closely. It is here that the vines of
great distinction — the Cabernet and Semillon of the
Gironde, the Rieslings and Traminer from the Rhine
and Moselle, and the others — come to their finest
bearing; it is only in these counties, as a matter of fact,
that they have ever been planted on any considerable
scale. The wines produced from them may never,
perhaps, have been noble, but they have at least been

71]

fine — the best in the European style that the United States could offer.

The vineyards of the Coast counties, however, have always been small as compared to those of the great interior valley. This valley, which extends down the length of California for four hundred miles, between the coastal ranges on the west and the Sierras on the east, is for purposes of convenience (and also because of certain differences in soil and climate) divided into the Sacramento Valley at the north, the San Joaquin Valley at the south, and the Central Valley in between. This enormous tract of land is the greatest raisin-producing region of the world, and the great table-grape region of the United States. Here, especially in the San Joaquin Valley, thousands upon thousands of acres are given over to the Muscat of Alexandria, the grape from which Muscat or Malaga [1] raisins are made, and which also yields a coarse and highly alcoholic sweet wine, with a bouquet which George Husmann, one of the early California vine-growers, once vaguely described as " leonine." The Muscat wine is passionately loved by the Italo-Americans; so much so that it might almost be called the Italo-American whisky. The San Joaquin Valley is also the principal growing-region for the Sultanina, usually called Thompson's Seedless, from which the seedless raisins

[1] The grape called Malaga in California, strangely enough, is not the grape which yields Malaga raisins. And incidentally, to increase the confusion, the grape called Malaga in California is not the grape from which the Spanish Malaga wines are made; the origin and correct name of the California Malaga are unknown.

are made. The Sultanina has also become very popular lately as a table grape, and during prohibition it has been used a good deal for making a dry white wine of no particular distinction. There is little rainfall in the San Joaquin, and not many years ago it was a baking desert; but with the diversion of the water from the Sierra watershed, and its distribution through an elaborate irrigation system, the rich soil of the valley has been made enormously productive. Unfortunately, however, irrigation and the production of fine wines do not go hand in hand. In the Central Valley the dominating grape is the Tokay, which is not the true Tokay wine grape of Hungary,[1] but an Arabian grape named Ahmar abu Ahmar, " Red father of Red." The Tokay is popular partly because it is pleasing to look at, partly because it has an iron constitution and is not upset by long rides in refrigerator cars, and partly because it has a crisp meaty texture and a neutral flavour. It is definitely not a wine grape. In the Sacramento Valley also this so-called Tokay is the dominating variety.

But in this inland valley large quantities of the less distinguished and more prolific wine varieties are also grown, and it is almost certain that if the United States ever becomes a wine-drinking nation, the cheap and wholesome wines which this region can produce so bountifully will become the staples of the trade. The soil is unbelievably fertile and yields prodigious crops, though many parts of the Central and Sacramento valleys, as well as the San Joaquin, require irrigation, and

[1] Which, by the way, is called Furmint and not Tokay.

it is ideally suited to the growing of such varieties as have been cultivated for years in the south of France and in Algeria, and from which the greater part of the commercial *vin ordinaire* is made. Scattered throughout its length there are also many acres where wines much better than ordinary may be grown, and there still exist vast stretches, particularly in the foot-hills of the Sierras, which have never yet come under the vine.

To the south, around Los Angeles, lies California's third great viticultural region. In general this district is much too hot for the production of good dry wines. It is here that the best of the highly alcoholic sweet and fortified wines have been made. Strangely enough, this district around Los Angeles also has the most considerable planting of Eastern grapes in all of California — principally of Concords — which are grown entirely to supply the tables of those retired Middle Westerners who have chosen Los Angeles to die in.

2

It was in this southern region that California's first vines were planted. Varieties of the European wine grape had been brought from Europe to Central America during the first years of the sixteenth century, and as early as 1524, when Cortez was Governor of Mexico, vines and cuttings were included in every cargo from Spain. They throve in Mexico, under the care of the padres; and as the line of missions advanced, the wine grape went along. In 1697 the Mission of Loreto was established on the peninsula of

Lower California, and this was followed by others, until a chain of them extended the whole length of the peninsula. Each new mission stemmed from one which had already been established, and each new mission vineyard stemmed from the established vines. The first vineyard in California proper was that of the Mission of San Diego, which was founded in 1769; the next earliest, that of San Gabriel, in 1771. Others followed, until the chain had reached well north of the present San Francisco.

For some reason, or more probably for a variety of reasons, these missions had but one grape, which not unnaturally came to be known as the Mission. Its characteristics are unlike those of any of the better-known European varieties, though there can be no question of its belonging to the species *vinifera*. Bioletti, the Professor of Viticulture at the University of California, says that it resembles very closely a grape that is grown in Sardinia, the Monica. It is pleasant to speculate by what tenuous thread of coincidence a grape of Sardinia should alone have reached California and have demonstrated its wine-growing possibilities. Its survival through all the vicissitudes of its long, slow journey is partly explained by the fact that it is a very vigorous and dependable grower and seems to thrive in California wherever it is given a root-hold. It is also partly explained by the special manner in which the California chain of missions was extended, each from its immediate predecessor. Had the missions been established independently, it seems likely that other varieties would have been introduced. The vigour of the Mission is very thoroughly demonstrated by certain famous individual vines. One of these, called the Trinity Vine, was planted on the property of the San Gabriel Mission in Los Angeles County in 1775, and still lives. Its trunk, just below the surface of the soil, is nine feet in circumference, and its arbour covers more than nine thousand square feet. Another, La Vina Grande, growing near the town of Carpenter in Santa Barbara County, had a somewhat more lively and strenuous career. It was planted in 1842, and it grew so rapidly that in a mere seventy-three years it covered a quarter-acre. Its greatest yield was in 1895, when it produced ten tons of grapes. Having burned the candle at both ends, it expired in 1915; and mournful citizens moved its enormous trunk to a place of honour near the highway which runs along the California coast, where it now stands embedded in a stately hunk of concrete. Throughout California there exist a number of vineyards and relics of vineyards which have been in bearing for three-quarters of a century or longer. The Californians have no compunctions, however, about uprooting an entire vineyard if they think that prunes will be more profitable; so these relatively ancient vineyards are not so common as they might otherwise be.

Chroniclers can hardly be blamed for having overworked the picturesque and sentimental aspect of the origin of the California industry, for it is beyond denial that throughout history the Church has been the chief and most passionate conservator of the vine. But it must be admitted that in California the contribution of the Franciscans is almost exclusively sentimental, beyond the bare demonstration that the European grape would grow there. Their wines were only mediocre, and naturally so, since they had much to do besides care for the vine, and it is significant that these wines entered hardly at all into the trade of those early days. The Mission, for all its sterling qualities as a plant, does not yield a first-rate wine, and though it is still used to some extent for the making of sweet wines, and to a lesser extent for dry white wines, it has been losing ground for many years before later arrivals of far better quality.

The first American settlers did not begin to arrive in California in considerable numbers until the forties, and even then were too busy seeking for gold to bother about the possibilities of the land itself. But behind the gold-seekers came not only the camp-followers, the riff-raff which is to be found wherever new land is opened up, but also a few of another type which is always to be found where new land is being opened — intelligent men so charged with a certain restless vigour, so much in need of constant action and constant change, that they cannot be happy save on the outermost fringe of civilization. Among these was a remarkable Hungarian, Count Augustin Haraszthy, who sowed the seeds of California's great viticultural industry almost single-handed. Haraszthy was a member of the minor Hungarian nobility [1] who emigrated

---

[1] Mr. August W. Derleth, of Sauk City, Wisconsin, has very kindly provided me with material about Haraszthy, including a reprint of a scarce pamphlet concerning the man.

to America in the spring of 1840. He and his companion had intended to settle in Florida, but on shipboard they changed their plans and decided to settle in Wisconsin instead. They reached what is now Sauk City and established themselves, and the impact of Haraszthy upon the community was immediate and lasting. To say that he ran things in that region would be to err on the side of understatement; his commanding bearing and fierce mustachios, his picturesque clothing, his powers as a mighty hunter, and his boiling enthusiasm were irresistible. He caused the town to be platted and gave it a name and in partnership with an Englishman engaged in a dozen different enterprises. Two years later he returned to Hungary and brought out his wife, his three sons, Gaza, Attila, and Arpad, and his aged father and mother. He also found time to compose a two-volume book of memoirs. Almost the only enterprise that he did not take a stab at in the neighbourhood of Sauk City, apparently, was grape-growing, though he may even have tried that. But Haraszthy, despite his great physical vitality, had the asthma, and he decided finally to depart for a milder climate. In 1849 he turned his back upon Sauk City and started for California; and after a journey of some nine months he reached San Diego, then a wild frontier village. In San Diego he made as strong an impression as he had in Wisconsin. Within a year he was made sheriff and fought to subdue the Indians. In 1852 he was elected to California's General Assembly, in which body he promptly made himself a commanding figure. But though he represented San Diego ably for his term, he never returned there to live; his attention was diverted to San Mateo County, the county which forms the southern arm of the Golden Gate. It was then, apparently, that he began to meditate upon California's viticultural possibilities; for Haraszthy meditation was the brother of action, and he promptly arranged for the importation of some characteristic vines from Europe. The first one which he received was the Alexandria (Muscat of Alexandria), and he must therefore be accounted the father of California's present raisin industry, which is based almost entirely upon that grape. Then he received a half-dozen varieties from Hungary. Just what they were is now lost to the record, but it seems probable that one of them was the grape called Zinfandel, which in a comparatively short time ousted the Mission as the staple variety. The Zinfandel, a red-wine grape, is not known by that name in Hungary; if it is a corruption of the Hungarian Zierfahndler it is a double corruption, for the Zierfahndler is a white grape. During many years it was more extensively grown than any other grape, for the vine yields generous crops and good wine, and it is still very popular, especially among the Italo-Americans.

It has already been remarked that San Mateo is too chill and foggy for grapes, and Colonel Haraszthy (somewhere between Sauk City and California he ceased to be Count and became Colonel) quickly found that out. Undaunted, he looked about for more suitable land, and in 1856 he hit upon a tract in the Sonoma Valley, whither he removed his wife, his in-

creasingly numerous progeny, his father, the mild and
scholarly " Old General," and his effects. The discovery that the best of the Franciscan wines had come
from Sonoma doubtless had some influence on his
choice. He set to work with his sons, and within two
years he had a vineyard of 85,500 vines and a nursery
of 460,000 rooted cuttings. For a number of years
Colonel Haraszthy carried on almost single-handed.[1]
He distributed cuttings and vines with an almost fa-
natical generosity; he lectured, and he addressed papers to agricultural societies. But he had a good deal
of inertia to overcome. The report of the Patent Office for 1856 (this was the predecessor of the Department of Agriculture), though it treats of grapes and
wine-making at great length, makes no mention whatever of California. But there was no stopping the man,
and gradually he gathered about him a group of enthusiasts. By the end of the decade the interest in
grape-growing was fairly general. In 1861 he got the
State to establish a Viticultural Commission, and almost as a matter of course was appointed one of the
three commissioners; the other two, with the Colonel
around, were almost necessarily sleeping commissioners. Armed with his official title, and at his own expense, he promptly set forth upon a viticultural tour
of Europe. His son Attila accompanied him. Another
of his sons, Arpad, was established in an œnological
school in France.

The record of that whirlwind trip through Europe,

[1] Though he employed some Chinese labourers. He is said to have
been the first person in California to employ Chinese.

which Colonel Haraszthy caused to be published as a book upon his return, is so full of zest that it might almost have been written by a twentieth-century Californian. Its style, though perhaps lacking polish, at times attains an almost mystical exaltation, for he could not take a middle ground. He wrote, for instance: " I visited various parts of France, the Netherlands, Holland, Rhenish Prussia, Bavaria, Nassau, Baden, Switzerland, Spain, Italy and England. Various examinations confirmed my previous conviction that California is superior in all the conditions of soil, climate, and other natural advantages, to the most favored wine-producing districts of Europe."

The Colonel returned from his mad dash across Europe with something considerably more valuable than his heightened opinion of California; he brought two hundred thousand vines and cuttings, included among which were examples of practically all of the most important varieties of Europe. These he set out in nursery vineyards, then distributed through the State, in order to discover to what conditions of soil, temperature, and rainfall each variety responded best. Most of these have been reimported since, and there is no doubt that in his enthusiasm he made mistakes and confusions. Yet this, almost single-handed and in little more than a decade, endowed California with the fruit of two thousand years of European grape-growing. The ambitious wine-making enterprise which he founded was a commercial failure, for Haraszthy, in spite of his catalytic powers, was a poor business man; and it was not long after that that his name disappears from the annals of California.[1]

3

As a result of the Haraszthian hoopla, particularly the European trip and subsequent report, there was naturally a great spurt in California wine-making. The first *Annual Report* of the Department of Agriculture, published in the year 1862, and addressed, incidentally, to Abraham Lincoln, makes recognition of this by devoting several pages to California's wine-growing possibilities. The State's yield of grapes and wine increased steadily. By 1877 the vintage had reached the very considerable bulk of four million gallons. But most of the early wine-growers, though they shared the Colonel's enthusiasm, did not share his wisdom. They did not heed his caution that they make their haste slowly. They did not understand that nothing can take the place of patience and sound methods in this art. And the result was wine of a very inferior sort, and an industry that soon became notorious for its dubious and definitely fraudulent practices. The first wines to be shipped out of the State were just plain bad — badly fermented, of the wrong grapes, improperly aged, and poorly put up. Having conducted their fermentation in a rash and slapdash

[1] There is unfortunately no room to tell of his non-viticultural exploits in California, nor of his subsequent experiences in Nicaragua, where he first engaged in a large filibustering enterprise, then secured a grant of many thousands of acres for growing sugar-cane, and finally died a violent death in a swamp, some say in the jaws of an alligator.

manner, they found themselves with large quantities of diseased and undrinkable wine on their hands. Instead of consigning this, as they should have, to the distillery or the vinegar vat, they tried to dose it with artificial preservatives and pass it off as sound.

Having thus earned a bad name for themselves with their first assault upon the wine-drinking world,[1] the Californians then undertook other means of disposing of their wares. Much of it was shipped to France, where, being of generous alcoholic content, it was blended with the small wines produced in the Midi. It is a mistake to think that all French wines are good wines; a great deal of the French production has to be blended with wines from other parts. In Bordeaux and elsewhere the blend of California and Midi wines was bottled and finally found its way back to the undiscriminating markets of the United States, where it was passed off as French wine. Other California shippers, more sophisticated, did not bother to send their wines to France for the Gallic blessing, but did their labelling at home. Thousands of bottles were shipped to the East, in French boxes, nailed with French nails, in French straw, and provided with an assortment of French names. Thus they sought to get around their reputation for bad wines by concealing the paternity of their good wines also.

Conditions became so nearly intolerable that finally the better wine-growers banded together and in 1880

---

[1] The habit of sneering at California's wines, still fairly widespread, is a consequence of those early mistakes, which will probably not be lived down for very many years.

got the State Legislature to pass a Pure Wine Law, adequately implemented, for the purpose of wiping out the grosser types of fraud, eliminating the use of such dangerous substances as aniline dyes, salicylic acid, alum, and other chemical antiseptics, and defining such traditional and unexceptionable practices as fining and the use of tannin. But this law had its positive as well as its negative or regulatory purpose. Its title, " An Act for the Promotion of the Viticultural Interests of the State," indicates as much; and accordingly a State Board of Viticulture was set up for the dissemination of reliable information on viticulture, wine-making, cellar management, and trade practices. The University of California, also, was directed to undertake investigation and instruction in the more technical aspects of the art. This moderate and reasonable law had, of course, the adherence of every respectable wine-maker, for these all knew that without some curb on their unscrupulous brethren California could never throw off the bad odour which surrounded its earlier reputation.

The law had the effect of wiping out, very promptly, the more vicious types of adulteration, and the Board of Viticulture and the University did much to spread enlightenment. Under the able direction of Professor E. W. Hilgard, and with the co-operation of growers and wineries, thorough investigations into every phase of viticulture and wine-making were carried out, especially into the special problems of wine-making in hot climates, and on the basis of these a sound and very useful body of literature was brought into being. If Haraszthy founded this industry, Professor Hilgard and those who worked with him established it on a solid basis. In consequence of this work many California wineries became models of up-to-date practice. The California wines, freed of their taint if not entirely of the memory of it, began to offer stiff competition in the Eastern markets to the products of the wine-makers of New York, Ohio, and Virginia, who were working with native grapes, and also to the imported wines. The cost of this work to the State of California was nothing when balanced against the services which it rendered, not merely to the producers, but to the American stomach. It ought also to be remarked that one of Professor Hilgard's young assistants, bearing the title of Cellar Foreman, Ampelographer, and Botanist, was Frederic T. Bioletti. As Professor of Viticulture at California he carries on in the same tradition today, though his work in wine-making, for certain reasons of a legalistic character, is restricted. At the moment more than a hundred newly imported varieties, from Argentina, Corsica, China, Japan, Italy, Morocco, Palestine, Russia, Tunis, Algeria, Turkey, Austria, and Transcaucasia, are being grown, tested, and propagated under his direction.

During the era of reform which was inaugurated by the Act of 1880 the outline of California's viticulture began to be filled in and the advantages and limitations of each district to be understood more accurately. Naturally, a good many mistakes were made. Such things are not done overnight, for the vine does not begin to bear until it is three years old, and a cautious viticulturist will not commit himself as to the suitability of a variety for a given region in much less than twenty years. Many of the great viticultural stations in Europe which are specializing in the adaption of root-stocks to various soils will not release the results of their work that soon. Nevertheless, it was more and more apparent that the best of the dry wines would come from the Coast counties, and there certain vineyards began to stand out as definitely superior. The practice of estate bottling — which is the surest proof of pride in the making and good faith in the selling — was adopted by the proprietors of many of these better vineyards.

Between 1877 and 1895 the production jumped from 4,000,000 gallons to 15,000,000 gallons. A good deal of this never left the State — California has always been the great wine-drinking region of the United States — but the shipments to the Eastern states nevertheless kept on growing, and there even developed a modest foreign trade. Mexico was the first foreign nation to use the California wines, and was followed by Hawaii and the Central American countries, and then the Orient. There developed quite a trade with the West Indies. The first effort to break into Europe was made in 1880, before the era of reform had really got under way, when the bark *Stella* set forth upon its now notorious voyage to Germany laden with ninety-five thousand gallons of assorted California wines. The red wines, made from the Mission, were pronounced quite dreadful by everyone in Europe who tasted them; the white wines, both dry and sweet, were pronounced drinkable, but refused as being inexcusably expensive, considering their quality. Financially the venture was a complete flop, but it did have the effect of making Europe realize the existence of California. In confirmation of the theory that any advertising is good advertising, a modest demand for the California wines began to develop in Germany, Holland, Belgium, the Scandinavian countries, and Great Britain. By the end of the century they had established themselves in these markets, after a fashion. The growers and shippers entered their wines with dogged persistence in every International Exposition and duly received a share of blue ribbons.

The Californians, however, were beginning to discover that they had another enemy to fight besides their bad reputation. That was the phylloxera. It has already been said that this pest is a native of the United States east of the Rockies, and California did not acquire this pest from over the mountains until the great Haraszthian boom. Its very earliest appearance on the California scene was in 1858, in Sonoma County, not long after Haraszthy had established his first vineyard there; consequently it has long been assumed that the pest got to California from the eastern United States by way of Europe, on the presumably infested vines which Haraszthy imported. Yet during those early days many of the native American varieties were being brought to California from the East, and it may have come on them. At any rate, it got there, and

87]

it was greeted as it was in Europe. First it mystified, then it was lightly dismissed as a passing blight, then it was fought with oratory and indignation, and finally it aroused something approaching panic. But the panic never reached the intensity of that of Europe, for the phylloxera, though very serious, has never worked its destruction as rapidly in California as it does in Europe. Thanks to the richness of the soil, a vine is for a time able to throw out new roots almost as fast as its old ones are destroyed, and it not infrequently takes as much as twenty years to expire. Yet the phylloxera wrought great damage nevertheless, and it spread inexorably until now there are only a couple of counties, in the hot sandy desert region, where it is not well and no doubt permanently established. The only method of combating it, as in Europe, is by grafting vines on resistant roots; and the development of satisfactory root-stocks, as in Europe, has been the subject of long and painstaking inquiry.

But, thanks to the slower spread of the phylloxera and to these investigations, the fight against it was successfully maintained, and it did not seriously hinder the development of wine-growing. Certainly it destroyed no more vines than prohibition. The great test of the California wines was to be the Paris Exposition of 1900. Dr. Harvey W. (Pure Food) Wiley, the father of our food and drug laws, such as they are, was by that time deeply involved in his rites of purification. He determined, together with the American growers, to flaunt American wines under the very noses of the French and to show them what

wholesome wine really was. Dr. Wiley had been in-
vited to be a member of the wine jury, but this was
nevertheless packed for France; of the 81 members,
77 were French. At the doctor's urging, a collection
of our finest wines, some Eastern, but most of them
Californian, was brought together. After a series of
harrowing mishaps, including the freezing of a number of the entries, the collection finally got to France.
The wine jury was already hard at work on the
thirty-six thousand different wines which had been
submitted for competition from all parts of the world
— a task which would have made even Professor
Saintsbury pause in dismay.[1] The date set for the
tasting of the American wines was June 19. The
American delegation worked feverishly to set forth
in proper style the wines on which the reputation of
the Stars and Stripes would stand or fall, and on the
morning of the 19th everything was ready. The
wines were on the tables, the jury had assembled.
Then one of the delegates suddenly popped a resolution, which had been prepared without Doctor
Wiley's knowledge, to the effect that wines " from
France or from foreign countries with labels affixed
bearing a false indication of origin shall not be examined, and consequently not compete."

The resolution had obviously been produced in

[1] Professor Saintsbury, apologizing in his old age for not undertaking the history of wine which he had long contemplated, explained
that he had been deterred because " I should have had to drink more
good wine than would now be good for my pocket or perhaps even
my health, and more bad than I could contemplate without dismay
in my advancing years."

order to eliminate the entire American display, for even under the era of reform our growers and shippers were accustomed to give their wines such type names as Burgundy, Bordeaux, Sauterne, Chablis, etc. Dr. Wiley almost collapsed with surprise and chagrin, and in vain did his assistant explain in flowing French that these type names did not imply imitation. The resolution was adopted unanimously (Dr. Wiley not voting). The American wines were hastily withdrawn after this distressing contretemps, that the fight might go on at a more leisurely pace. Dr. Wiley was on pretty thin ice, it must be admitted, for a big pure-food man. But there was a lot to be said on his side of the argument. Burgundy in the United States does not mean a wine grown in that part of France, but merely a rich, generous, and deeply coloured red wine which will not stand dilution. Claret in California does not mean a wine from Bordeaux, but any dry red wine of lightish colour that is high in acid and tannin and stands dilution successfully. Rhine wine is not something grown on the banks of the Rhine, but an exceedingly dry white wine possessing the bouquet which is characteristic of the Riesling grapes. Dr. Wiley pressed his argument with great vigour, eloquence, and earnestness. The jury began to retreat before his salvos of moral indignation and finally agreed to examine the wines and rate them, but not actually and officially to give awards. So the jurors fell once more to their smelling and tasting and peering, and in no time at all a generous proportion of the wines were rated as deserving gold, silver, and bronze medals and honourable mention, even though they were not formally to receive these honours.

This was probably the severest blow to their pride that the reformed wine-makers of California had ever received. Yet, in a way, it was flattery. For it was obvious that the preponderantly French jury had set out, in that engaging French way, to do a dirty trick. The Californians, characteristically, managed to turn the insult into a compliment. As Mr. Henry Lachman, one of the exhibitors, wrote some time later:

" There is no question that the wine produced in California comes nearer to the European product than that produced in any other country in the New World. We are convinced of this by the action of the jury at the Paris Exposition in putting out of competition all California wines bearing labels designating their types, which the French considered as imitations, although they had allowed these same labeled wines to enter into competition for the last twenty years."

Dr. Wiley also managed to put the experience to a practical use, for when he got home, he composed an official document, filled with the most subtly contrived distinctions, in which he undertook both to defend the American practice against the French and to urge the Americans to cut loose from it in order to avoid all possible reproach of imitation. Yet this proved to be more easily talked about than done, for the *demand* has always been predominantly for wines of European type and the demand refused to change at Dr. Wiley's urging. Wine-makers, like

91]

194

literary gentlemen, get small comfort out of their produce if they can get no one to swallow it. Mr. Charles A. Wetmore, another of the distinguished wine-makers of the last generation and long a member of the Viticultural Commission, put it very neatly in one of his reports, when he said:

" Whenever foreigners — and I include New York as among the most foreign people we have to deal with — will become satisfied with the best that each of our districts can produce without any attempt to imitate European styles, it will be time for them to complain that we do not produce typical California wines; but so long as the markets demand styles like favorite European brands, so long must California producers and dealers make attempts to please them, either with ignorantly devised methods and blends, or false labels."

Yet even this explanation has its weakness. For when all is said and done, California's wines are *naturally* after the European style. However important the influences of soil and climate may be, the best wines made from, say, the Semillon in California must still have a family resemblance to the wines made from the same grape in the Sauternes district. The stubborn fact is that California wines are, and always will be, " imitations " of the European types — until such time as the Californians develop unique and distinctive vines of their own.

4

So in spite of Dr. Wiley's brilliant logical counterpoint, the uproar attending the 1900 Exposition did not, actually, alter the course of California viticulture at all. The growers continued to make their Margaux Souvenir, their Special Burgundy, their Chablis Type, their Château This and That, and so on. In 1895 the total production in California was 17,000,000 gallons; by 1909 it had jumped to around 50,000,000 gallons. The wine-production never went higher than that, though exports continued to show a moderate but comforting annual increase. Long since, the California wines had taken first place over the wines produced by native grapes in the East.

Then the growers and makers of wines began to feel the effect of a plague which was far more serious than anything with which they had had to contend — a plague much more dreadful than the phylloxera. I mean, of course, the plague of prohibition. Books have been written on the origin and diffusion of this disease, and its pathology; and I shall not go into that painful subject here, since it seems at last to be healing itself anyway. But the wine-makers treated it just as they did the phylloxera: first dismissing it lightly as being of too little importance to bother about, then speaking of it with indignation, and finally growing panic-stricken as it marched relentlessly from one victory to another. State after state was closed to the wine-makers; gradually their market melted away. By 1915 the wine-men had their backs to the wall; and

I know of no reading that is more affecting than the reports of the International Congress of Viticulture which was held concurrently with the Panama-Pacific International Exposition in 1915.[1] To begin with, the nations of Europe were already embroiled in that war which was to end war, and most of the wine-men who were to have been delegates were either fighting each other in the trenches or had already been killed. Only three foreign delegates attended: Dr. Cleonthes Vassardakis, representing Greece, who lived in this country anyway and who contributed a few non-controversial remarks about Bacchus; Mr. I. Nagasawa, representing Japan, which makes no wine, who had for years lived in California; and one Rossati, an Italian, who read a paper on a method of using grape stems in the manufacture of paper. The rest were Americans, most of them old friends anyway; and the theme which ran through everything that they had to say was the rising menace of prohibition, how to stop it, how to make people realize that wine is the greatest friend of temperance and the innocent victim of the prejudice against liquors. Resolutions were passed denouncing prohibition as " virtual confiscation of property without payment," and plans for campaigns of " public education " were gloomily discussed. Yet most of the delegates knew, even then, that the days of their industry were numbered.

Finally, the prohibitionists won their battle, and

[1] *Official Report of the Session of the International Congress of Viticulture*, held in Recital Hall, Panama-Pacific International Exposition, San Francisco, July 12 and 13, 1915.

the vine-growers were thrown into a panic. Thousands of acres of excellent vines were grubbed up and the laxative and familiar prune planted in their places. The Eighteenth Amendment was written into law, and the California growers and vintners found themselves with large stocks of mature and aging wine in their cellars, representing much labour and a very considerable investment. The deadline was January 16, 1920, and the official ruling was that all wine for export must be on board ship and actually out of port on that day. During the late months of 1919 shipments for export jumped tremendously. On December 31 a million-dollar shipment of wine left San Francisco on a Dollar liner, bound for the Orient. It contained ten thousand cases of sparkling wines and about seven thousand barrels of California's finest still wines.

Thus, after a short and exciting life of little more than sixty years — little more, that is, than the life of a good sherry — California's wine-making industry was ruthlessly destroyed. When prohibition became the law, California had, according to the *California Grower*, some 700 wineries. Of these, 520 were in the Coast counties — 256 in Sonoma County, 120 in Napa County, and the rest divided largely between Santa Clara, Contra Costa, Alameda, Mendocino, and Santa Cruz. In the interior valleys there were some 158 wineries; and in southern California there were 22, many of these being of huge capacity and controlling the vintage of enormous areas. A few remain. Some held on for a year or two as bonded wineries and warehouses, then passed out of existence; many of them sold their equipment intact to the great *bodegas* of the province of Mendoza in Argentina. With the disappearance of these went many proud names — Gundlach-Bundschu, William Hoelscher, Lachman and Jacobi, Cresta Blanca, A. Finke's Widow, Charles Krug, and others. Some of these may one day be revived; others are gone for ever.

But though prohibition meant death to California's efforts to produce wines of real breed and distinction, it actually brought a new prosperity to many growers of wine grapes. Its effect on the economic status of California's vineyardists is one of the most grotesque and ridiculous chapters in the whole farcical story. Prohibition has proved merely to be a ban on fine wines. Congress had left a loop-hole which allowed the making of wines at home. So instead of selling their grapes to the wineries, many of the growers had the enterprise to load them into refrigerator cars and ship them east, especially to the big cities with large foreign-born populations. And here developed another surprise. The amateur wine-makers of the East knew nothing of the differences between one grape and another; they knew only the distinction between " black " grapes and " white " grapes, that one made red wine and the other white. It is notorious that the best wine grapes are not the most beautiful, so these amateurs walked right by them in the markets and leaped upon the prettiest. The small and spotted Cabernet, the undistinguished-looking Pinot, the thin-skinned and sticky Riesling and Semillon — these went begging, while the coarse and abundant varieties, with thick skins and placid dispositions, were snapped up hastily. The result was an almost complete reversal in the order of prices. The grapes which brought high prices — from a dollar and a half to two dollars and more for a twenty-four-pound "lug" — were the common black varieties, such as Zinfandel, Alicante Bouschet, Carignane, Mataro, Grenache — all good, sound, reliable red-wine grapes, but capable of yielding nothing like a really fine wine. Their wines, as the French say, are for *consommation* and not for *dégustation*. Before prohibition they brought from twelve to eighteen dollars a ton, practically never more.

So the bulk vineyards flourished, and the growers who had laboured for quality — few know the difficulties to be overcome and the number of enemies to be met and conquered before a vintage of the finest grapes is successfully achieved — were forced to cut down their noble plants and graft the cheap and highly productive varieties upon their roots. Under prohibition California's annual production of wine grapes has just about doubled, and only the conscientious growers of fine vines have been penalized.

But for three factors we might find ourselves today with no fine vines at all. One is the outrageous and unreasonable love which some growers hold for their finest vines — a love which is everywhere evident in Europe, less evident in California, but which makes the destruction of the vine seem akin to fratricide. Such growers will starve rather than give up their vines. Another of these factors is of course the steady demand for sacramental wines. Some of the clergy appear to find the light white wines of the Rhenish type best suited to their sacred mysteries, whilst others detect a special efficacy in the light clarets and mellow burgundies. Still another group will use none but the lush and heavily fortified liquorous wines from the south, the so-called ports and sherries. Thanks to these differences of opinion, the Church has once more proved itself a faithful and catholic friend of the vine. The third was the rise and growth of the concentrate industry, with the assistance of the Federal Government. The technique of concentrating grape juices by evaporation or by freezing had long been known, and it is used in many parts of the world in the making of some kinds of sweet wines. The growers banded together and called themselves Fruit Industries, Ltd., and secured a loan of three million dollars from the Federal Government. The idea was that through this selling agency these concentrates might be sold to amateurs, who in turn could dilute them to the original consistency of the juice and allow them to ferment in the privacy of their hall closets. Then, thanks largely to the legal dexterity of Mrs. Mabel Walker Willebrandt, a technique for " servicing " these concentrates was worked out. It became possible to place one's order with a salesman, who installed the diluted concentrate of whatever type might be desired, inoculated it with a culture of pure wine yeast, and presided over its

[98

fermentation, finally filtering, bottling, capping, and labelling the wine which was thus made. The rise of this industry naturally brought some relief to those stubborn fools who had refused to sacrifice their good vines.

At the present time the viticulturists of California are utterly confused. In June of 1932 there were about 7,000,000 gallons of dry wines and 8,000,000 gallons of sweet wines in the bonded cellars. Encouraged by the growth of anti-prohibition sentiment, the Californians in 1932 made some 10,000,000 additional gallons (which, however, must be given a decent opportunity to mature). All of this put together is only about half of one year's demand in the years prior to prohibition. It is much less than half if the sensational increase in wine-drinking under prohibition is taken into account. So when real wine is legalized, the Californians will have to start from scratch; there will not be enough wine to satisfy the demand. The stop-gap legalization of " 3.2 per cent wine " has had the effect of still further confounding their confusion. There is not, and never has been, any such thing as a 3.2 per cent wine; to legalize such a beverage — several brands of 3.2 per cent " pop," made out of wine, water, and carbon dioxide gas, are already on the market — is merely, again, to penalize those who seek to produce pure, sound, healthy wines and to favour the not too scrupulous merchant who will produce anything that he can sell. Not until Congress allows the making and selling of the pure and naturally fermented juice of the grape, without idiotic specifications as to the precise degree of alcoholic content, will California be allowed to resume its place as one of the world's great wine-growing regions.

Chapter Four

ON THE MAKING OF WINES

WINE-MAKING, when stripped down to its bare essentials, is simple and easy. Grapes are crushed and are put, skins and all, in a clean open receptacle. If this mess of crushed grapes, which is usually called *must*, is left in a fairly warm place and let alone it will presently begin to ferment. The fermentation, which is signified by gentle gurglings and writhings, continues for several days, or even for a week or so. When there are no further signs of travail, the new turgid wine is pressed free of the solid matter and placed in another container and lightly stoppered. This new wine continues to ferment, but much more gently, sometimes for a month and sometimes for several months. At the end of that time the clear wine is separated from the rest of the solid matter, which has sunk to the bottom of the receptacle, and may be drunk. Given clean receptacles, suitable grapes, and the assistance of a benign Providence, one may thus procure a drinkable, if not exciting, vinous beverage. The boiling of an egg is not much simpler.

The whole art and science of wine-making is only

101]

an elaboration of that primitive method. Œnology is a highly developed branch of applied organic chemistry, yet the chemist with his refinements and his analyses seeks only to remove the uncertainty from the natural process, by assuring a regular and perfect fermentation and by eliminating the obstacles which otherwise a new wine must overcome before it reaches a sound and gracious maturity. Engineers and their devices, beginning with the learned Archimedes, have contributed important improvements to the art of wine-making, but the best of these improvements are no more than extensions of the human hand and foot and refinements upon the primitive fermenting-vat. The whole difference, in short, between primitive wine-making and enlightened wine-making is that the former was laborious for the wine-maker and uncertain in its result, the latter less laborious (especially if the wine is being made in large quantities) and more certain. Superb wines and very nasty wines have been, and are being, made in both ways.

Since wine-making, even in the most elaborate winery, is still at bottom a natural process, the differences between one wine and another — and no two natural wines are exactly alike — have their origin chiefly in the grapes from which they are made. A good wine grape must possess certain definite qualities. A grape which lacks one or more of these properties (such as the ordinary Concord) will not yield a good wine, no matter how careful the wine-maker may be. But above and beyond these indispensable qualities, each species and variety of grape has unique qualities of its own which impart a special and highly individual character to the wine which is made from it. The Pinot Noir, and no other vine, yields wine of the true Burgundy characteristics. The Cabernet, and no other, yields that special flavour and bouquet which are found in the finest red wines of the Médoc. It is the variety of grape (plus the very important differences which soil and climate may make in the same variety) that determines the bouquet, the flavour, the vinosity, the lightness or depth of colour, the rapidity with which the wine matures, its longevity, and even, to some extent, its susceptibility to disease. The first business of the wine-maker is consequently to secure grapes which are *wine* grapes — not table grapes, nor grape-juice grapes, nor cooking grapes, but those which experience and the laboratory have both shown to be suitable for wine.

ANATOMY OF THE WINE GRAPE

The *special* qualities of the various kinds of grape which are available to American wine-makers will be discussed later. Before going into the differences between wine grapes it seems reasonable to examine first those qualities which they have in common. The three parts of the grape are the seeds, the skin, and the pulp, in an ascending order of importance. The stems also play a part in the making of many red wines.

Seeds. The only substance in the seeds which is valuable to the wine-maker is the tannin, which forms about ten per cent of their weight and is partly extracted from the seeds during the course of fermentation. Tannin is one of the indispensable elements in wine. A wine which is deficient in tannin is very temperamental and apt to fly off the handle on the slightest provocation. A wine which contains plenty of tannin, on the other hand, resists disease, becomes clear and bright with little or no assistance, and has a more brilliant colour. A wine which contains an excess of tannin is astringent when young, and causes the mouths of all but Italians to pucker a little. But this youthful brashness disappears with advancing age, and the wine is all the more mellow and generous for it.

Grape seeds contain from ten to eighteen per cent of oil, from which a superior soap may be made and which is used in some countries as fuel for wick lamps. The seeds also contain certain volatile acids in very small quantities, which, like the oil, are essential to the germination of the seed, but can give a thoroughly unpleasant taste to the wine. These substances do not make their way into the wine, however, unless the seeds are broken during the crushing of the grapes. That almost never happens if reasonable care is used.

Skin. The skins of grapes have many substances to contribute to the wine. Like the seeds, they contribute a good deal of tannin.

It is in the skin that the colouring matter of the grape is to be found exclusively (though in certain varieties, called *teinturiers,* there is also pigment in the pulp). This pigment consists of a whole complex of substances called enolic acids, the exact nature of which is still obscure; it is known, though, that the complex varies according to the variety of grape. From the point of view of the wine-maker, the pigment has one very definite characteristic: it is only slightly soluble in the fresh must at ordinary temperatures, but is dissolved by the alcohol which is developed during fermentation.[1] For this reason, in making red wines the juice is always fermented on the skins. Another point of practical importance is the fact that the pigment is oxidized by prolonged contact with the air, and after being oxidized is not soluble in alcohol; therefore grapes which are left hanging overlong on the vines yield wines which are somewhat less deeply coloured than those from grapes which are gathered at the peak of their maturity.

The skins also contain, in varying quantities according to the variety, certain aromatic substances which give a definite character to the wine. In most *vinifera* wine grapes this aroma is slight; but in some, particularly Cabernet, Riesling, and the Muscat varieties, it is pronounced. The aroma of Cabernet and Riesling is much admired; that of Muscat is not. Most of the American species have these aromatic substances in greater or less degree, that of Delaware being fragrant and agreeable, that of Concord, Niagara and many others being abhorrent to most wine-makers. The

[1] The pigment may be dissolved in the fresh juice by heating to 120° F. That is the way bottled grape juice gets its colour.

105]

aroma should not be confused with bouquet. The bouquet, which appears only after the wine is made, arises from quite other substances.

The skin of the ripe grape is coated with a thin film of waxy substance, whitish or greyish in colour, which is called the bloom. This does not itself contribute anything to the wine, but it is very important nevertheless, for the yeasts which float about in the air at vintage season are trapped and held by the bloom. Without yeasts there could be no fermentation. Unfortunately the bloom also traps other things which do the wine no good, such as certain undesirable " wild " yeasts, harmful bacteria, moulds, dust, and insecticides. The wine-maker must face the fact that these exotic substances, if they are allowed to, are capable of contributing special, and unattractive, qualities to the wine.

Pulp. The pulp of the grapes provides the great bulk of the material which eventually becomes wine. In some varieties (eating varieties) it is crisp and compact; in most wine varieties it is very soft and juicy. The chemical composition of the pulp is very involved, and it differs tremendously, not only from one variety to another, but from season to season in the same vineyard according to the vagaries of the weather and the cultivator — and, of course, according to the state of ripeness of the grape. The juice from the squeezed pulp of " average " ripe dry-wine grape consists, roughly, of the following ingredients:

	Per cent
Water	77.
Fermentable sugar	20.
Free acids (tartaric, malic, etc.)	.60
Potassium bitartrate	.63
Mineral salts (sulphates, phosphates, etc.), fats, nitrogenous compounds, pectic substances, and traces of other substances	1.77
	100.00

This is admittedly a skeletal table of contents of the juice from the pulp of an " average " dry-wine grape, but it is sufficiently detailed for anyone but an organic chemist. The points to be remembered are that the water and sugar together constitute 97 per cent of it, that all the other substances, however important, come to no more than 3 per cent, and that tannin is conspicuous by its absence.

The percentage of sugar which the juice contains is of vital importance, because the percentage of alcohol in the finished wine is directly proportional to it. The sugar is normally converted, with the help of the yeast ferments, into almost equal quantities of carbon dioxide (CO_2) and alcohol (C_2H_5OH). Thus, fresh grape juice containing 20 per cent sugar produces a wine having about 10 per cent of alcohol. That is the first rule of wine-making. *Two degrees of sugar give one degree of alcohol.*

Experience has shown that yeasts, under the most favourable circumstances, will not continue their work of fermentation in an alcoholic solution of more than 14 or 15 per cent, even though there is still plenty of sugar to work on. Consequently a must containing more than 28 per cent of sugar (remember the two-to-one rule) cannot be expected to yield a dry wine; it will always contain an excess of unfermented sugar. And on the other hand experience has shown that a finished wine containing less than 8 per cent of alcohol is not only a thin and unpalatable beverage, but an exceedingly sickly and unstable mixture. That is a fact which advocates of " 3.2 per cent wines " seem never able to get through their heads. In short, both grapes which are deficient in sugar and those which have an excess of sugar are unsatisfactory for dry, natural wines. The best results are to be had when the sugar content is between 20 and 24 per cent.

The ingredients other than sugar and water, though present in only small quantities, have important roles in the process of fermentation and in the composition of the finished wine. Some enter directly into the complex reactions of fermentation, and so are transformed into other substances; some play no part in the fermentation, but enter into the finished wine unchanged. The bulk of them are either acids or acid salts, and in practice they are lumped together as "total acids."

The acidity of the juice is important, first, because it helps to assure a sound fermentation. The yeasts which transform the must into wine work best in an acid solution. Fresh grapes carry on their skins, in addition to the yeasts of vinous fermentation, a host of ferments of disease, deposited from the air, which may hinder the sound fermentation or even overpower the good yeasts and spoil the wine entirely. An acid solution inhibits these ferments; a neutral solution favours their propagation.

In the second place, a considerable degree of acidity in the juice means a considerable degree of acidity in the finished wine, and a wine to be sound and healthy must have sufficient acidity. (By acidity is not meant the presence of acetic acid, or vinegar, which is a product of bad fermentation and is always a sign of sickness in the wine.) A wine that lacks sufficient acid is flat to the taste and relatively short-lived.

Third, the full colour of a red wine is best brought out in an acid solution.

Finally, the acids of the wine contribute, in ways which are still only partly understood, to the development of the wine's bouquet.

Stems. The grape stems are frequently crushed along with the grapes. If they are dry and woody, they contribute little to the wine. If they are soft and pulpy, however, they yield a large quantity of tannin.

It ought to be said once again that this analysis of wine grapes is of " average " fruit, and that the chemical composition of two batches of grapes is practically never the same. Indeed, the composition of any given grape varies steadily as it ripens on the vine. At first it is very high in acid and low in sugar.

Gradually, as it ripens, the proportion of sugar increases and that of the acid decreases. Finally it reaches a maximum of sugar content and is ripe. But the *proportion* of sugar to the total weight of the grape may be increased still further by allowing the grapes to hang on the vine until they are overripe, since as they begin to shrivel, a certain quantity of the water evaporates. It is in this way that certain of the very sweet and liquorous wines are made.[1] But such curiosities are out of the province of this book. A sweet wine may be all right occasionally, but it will never do for a steady diet; and in any case the making of it is a distinct and special art.

THE FERMENTATION

Before much was known of the chemical composition of grapes, and of the roles which the various constituents play in the fermentation, the wine-maker had to judge entirely by taste and appearance when the grapes were ready for the vintage. With experience a person may grow skilful at this, but for the novice this method is quite out of the question. The sweetness of grapes, as it seems to one who eats them, can be very deceptive, for the sensation of sweetness need have no relation to the grape's actual richness of sugar. Some grapes may be comparatively low in sugar, yet seem sweet merely because they are also low in acidity. Some grapes taste harsh and sour because of their richness in acid, when actually they may have plenty of sugar.

[1] And also the way raisins are made.

Wine-makers, therefore, do not rely upon experience alone; they are able to tell by very simple tests, which will be described in their proper place, just what degree of sugar and what degree of acidity their grapes possess, so that the vintage may be conducted just when the grapes are at their prime. In parts of Europe the day of the vintage is set by a village committee and published by the mayor, and it is an offence to gather the grapes before that day. The vintage, in all wine-drinking countries, is a time of gaiety and a time of hard work. For the bulk of the grapes, naturally, reach their full ripeness at about the same time; and they must be gathered, save under exceptional conditions, before that prime is passed, and converted as quickly as possible into the new wine. In Europe the men, women, and children are all pressed into the work in order to get it done in the quickest possible time. In California the vintage is made by families of itinerant " pickers " who begin with the cherries in the early summer and work at one crop after another, concluding late in the fall with the last of the second-growth vineyards. They live in the open, in tents, and they are of every nationality — Japanese, Chinese, Mexicans, Italians, and others. Strangely enough, few French are to be found, either as labourers or as proprietors, in the vineyards of California. In Europe, where the tradition of making the wine where it is grown is still strong, the grapes are gathered in baskets, carried to wagons, and by these hauled directly to the crushers or, in those few places where the foot is still the prevailing crusher, to the treading-floor or vat.

On the great estates the crusher is of course a part of the property. The smaller proprietors frequently use a crusher owned by one of the neighbouring farmers, who trundles it from farm to farm just as a thresher goes the rounds on our Middle Western farms. In the great mass-vintages of Algeria and the Midi the work is entirely mechanized from the picking on; sometimes there are even narrow-gauge railways to carry the grapes from vineyards to winery. In California before prohibition the greater part of the wine was made in large central wineries, and the grapes were carried to these in boxes, by truck. Occasionally the grapes were loaded directly onto open flat-cars and sent overnight by rail. The amateur wine-maker who sprang into being during prohibition and who makes his wine at home finds his excitement, not in the actual vintage, but in a daily reading of the produce reports and in frequent visits to the wholesale produce markets, for those who are so fortunate as to be able to grow their own grapes are few compared to those who depend upon the market. Yet even this intrusion of the marts of trade is not without its thrills, for the better varieties of grapes have a way of appearing in the market suddenly and disappearing just as suddenly; the problem is to catch them. But this problem of finding and choosing the proper grapes will be discussed more fully in the chapters devoted specifically to the making of white wine and red wine.

After the grapes are gathered (or bought) the first step is the crushing. In some few wine-making regions, as for instance parts of the valley of the Douro and its tributaries, where real port comes from, this crushing is still done by the traditional method of treading. The grapes are emptied on great treading-floors by processions of carriers who come marching to music from the vineyards, bearing their baskets of grapes on their shoulders. The treading is done, frequently, to more music — to that of concertina, flute, and bass drum. The treading becomes even a sort of stately dance, the elaborate figures of which are gone through with the high seriousness of acolytes engaged in a religious ceremony. Some practical advantages are claimed for this primitive means of crushing the grapes, of which the most important are the thorough aeration of the freshly crushed grapes and the avoidance of all danger of crushing seeds. The disadvantages are obvious.

In most wineries today the crushing is done by machine, the grapes being run between the rollers of great power crushers, from which the must is pumped or descends by gravity to the fermenting-vats. By tradition, the vats must be made of the choicest white oak; and in cellars of great age, in Europe, they are sometimes elaborately carved and highly polished. More often they are not carved, but they are superb pieces of cooperage none the less. In California, where oak is scarce, the fermenting-vats are frequently made of redwood. In wineries devoted to the production of vast quantities of ordinary wine, wood is sometimes replaced by vats of vitrified brick or cement or glass-lined steel. The principal virtue of these kinds of vat is that they are easy to cleanse and keep clean —

a matter of the very highest importance in wine-making.

It is not until the must is in the vats that the yeasts, which are charged with the high duty of transforming the fresh juice into wine, begin their mysterious work. Although much has been learned of the nature of fermentation since the time of Pasteur, there still remain many steps in the process of alcoholic fermentation which no man understands. It was not until 1857, when Pasteur initiated his great series of researches leading to the discovery and isolation of the living organisms called wine yeasts, and definitely linked their vital processes with fermentation, that it was really understood at all. It was he who demonstrated that in wine-making the fermentation always proceeds in the presence of living yeasts. He embodied his conclusion in the famous observation that: "the chemical act of fermentation is essentially a phenomenon correlative with a vital act, commencing and ceasing with the latter. I am of opinion that alcoholic fermentation never occurs without simultaneous organization, development, multiplication of cells, or the continued life of cells already formed. . . . *If I am asked in what consists the chemical act whereby the sugar is decomposed and what is its real cause, I reply that I am completely ignorant of it*" (italics mine).

The priests of chemistry who held sway at that time attacked this heretical doctrine by satire, by ridicule, and by logical demonstrations which were marvels of deductive reasoning. For his conclusions were truly revolutionary — how much so may be gleaned from an essay on wine-making which was printed in the annual report of the U. S. Commissioner of Patents [1] in the same year as Pasteur's first great discovery, 1857. Nowhere in the essay is it suggested that organisms are involved in the process; the word " yeast " is not used. Pasteur's discoveries were the real beginning of knowledge of the process of fermentation; and so thoroughly did he demonstrate his contentions that even the academic chemists were forced finally to come round. That Pasteur carried his work far beyond this and contributed more to knowledge of fermentation than any other man is a matter for no argument. In America he is best known for his contributions to medicine and as the father of pasteurized milk; in France he is revered as the man who brought light into the dark places of traditional wine-making practices.

From Pasteur's time on, the secret of the mechanism of alcoholic fermentation has steadily yielded before the researches of investigators. Pasteur concentrated attention upon the organisms present in all fermenting liquids. The next great discovery, by Buchner in 1897, appeared superficially to cancel the discoveries of Pasteur; for Buchner found that fermentation is caused, not by the yeast itself, but by a substance which the yeast secretes. Buchner was engaged on experiments having to do with a totally different question, and had some occasion to prepare

[1] The Patent Office was the parent of our Department of Agriculture.

a liquid from yeast, by crushing and filtering the cells, which were entirely free of all traces of living cellular matter. This liquid, to his astonishment, proceeded to cause fermentation in a sugar solution. The experiment on which he was working was spoiled by this unexpected fermentation. But he had stumbled upon a very important discovery. For, actually, it was a partial answer to the question which Pasteur had begged when he said: "If I am asked in what consists the chemical act whereby the sugar is decomposed and what is its real cause, I reply that I am completely ignorant of it." He had shown that fermentation is a chemical process which can be carried out in the absence of the living yeast cell, since the active agent in fermentation is a *secretion* of the yeast cell and not the yeast itself. Buchner called that substance *zymase*.

Stated in its simplest terms, then, alcoholic fermentation consists of the breaking-down of sugar into alcohol and carbon dioxide in the presence of zymase:

$$C_6H_{12}O_6 \xrightarrow{\text{(zymase)}} 2\ C_2H_5OH + 2\ CO_2$$
$$\text{(sugar)} \qquad\qquad \text{(alcohol)} \quad \text{(carbon dioxide)}$$

Buchner's discovery had the same effect on biochemists that the scent of an escaped convict is supposed to have on a bloodhound. They have been following ever since the trail which he pointed. It is needless to tell of their discoveries on the way.[1]

[1] Those who are interested in the detailed chemistry of fermentation will find it set forth in the standard book on the subject, *Alcoholic Fermentation*, by Arthur Harden; revised edition, 1932.

Summed up, they are: first, that the zymase which Buchner found is not one single activating substance, but a large and still only partially understood complex of substances, each of which has its part to play in the mechanism of fermentation; and, second, that the transformation is not a simple breaking-down of the molecules of sugar into the molecules of alcohol and carbon dioxide, but a succession of breakings-down, that the " conversion of sugar into alcohol and carbon dioxide during the process of fermentation is most probably the result of a series of reactions, during which various intermediate products are momentarily formed and then used up in the succeeding state of the process." [1]

The fermentation which takes place in grape must is of course much more involved than that which takes place in controlled laboratory experiments, since the composition of the must not only is variable, but is made up of many other substances besides sugar, some of which undergo change along with the fermentation. The nature of these accessory changes — and it is these, after all, that are responsible for the infinite variety of wines — is still pretty much a matter of guess-work.

The problem is made still more intricate by the fact that true vinous fermentation is only one of many different kinds of fermentation, and that there are many species and varieties of yeast (torulas, and " wild " yeasts) whose ferments are capable of producing not only *sound* vinous fermentation, but fer-

[1] Harden, p. 109.

mentation which is harmful and even completely destructive. The whole process of fermentation, in wine-making, may be summed up as a struggle between the good yeasts, which seek to transform the must into wine, and those bad organisms which seek to prevent the successful transformation.

The family of the *Saccharomyces*, of which there are several species and innumerable varieties or strains, is the one to which all good wine yeasts belong. (It is also the family to which all good beer yeasts belong.) The most important of the wine yeasts is that species called *Saccharomyces ellipsoideus*,[1] so named because under the microscope it is shown to be elliptical in shape. The spores of this yeast hibernate in the ground during the winter, but as summer advances, they are distributed through the air, being carried hither and thither by every vagrant breeze. As the grapes ripen, the yeasts are deposited upon their skins in great numbers, and by vintage time not only the grapes themselves but the vines and the foliage are covered with them. Finally, when the grapes are crushed and placed in the fermenting-vats, these yeasts, in company with many other microscopic organisms, find themselves in a medium which is very favourable to their propagation. Normally the con-

---

[1] Two other species, *S. apiculatus* and *S. pasteurianus*, are normally found in freshly crushed grape must. *S. apiculatus* multiplies very rapidly and is most evident early in the course of fermentation; *S. pasteurianus* is more evident at the end of fermentation, helping to " clean up " the remaining traces of unfermented sugar. *S. ellipsoideus* does the great bulk of the work.

ditions are more favourable to the propagation of the wine yeasts than of the other organisms. The yeasts begin immediately to grow and to reproduce themselves by budding and separating, so that in a remarkably short time their number has increased beyond all belief. During the life of the yeast the sugar of the grape must enters the yeast cell through its walls, and there, in the presence of the zymase which the yeast secretes, it undergoes that involved series of reactions which ends only when each molecule of sugar has been transformed into almost equal quantities of alcohol and carbon dioxide. Actually, each hundred parts of sugar gives slight quantities of other substances besides alcohol and water; Pasteur gives the following estimate:

Alcohol	48.4
Carbon dioxide	46.6
Glycerine	3.2
Succinic acid	0.6
To the yeast	1.2
	100.0

And under practical (as distinct from laboratory) conditions there are slight quantities of many other substances. But for practical purposes it is sufficiently accurate to say that a given quantity of sugar yields almost equal quantities of alcohol and carbon dioxide. Each cell is a separate factory for the production of these two compounds. The more cells there are, the faster the fermentation takes place and the less danger there is of interference from the dangerous organisms which have also gone into the must. The speed of fermentation, other things being equal, is exactly proportional to the number of yeast cells. For this reason wine-makers always try to encourage the rapid multiplication of the good yeasts at the very start.

In encouraging this rapid growth, wine-makers take advantage of the fact that yeasts behave quite differently when they are in the presence of an abundant supply of air from what they do when air is denied them. When they have plenty of air, the yeasts reproduce themselves with tremendous speed, but make little alcohol; when air is denied them, they do not reproduce themselves so rapidly, but their efficiency as makers of alcohol is greatly increased. That is why, during crushing and treading, the grapes are allowed complete contact with the air, and that is why the must is always exposed to the air during the first part of fermentation (but lightly covered, of course, to keep out flies and dust). That also provides scientific justification for the practice, which prevails in some parts of the Bordeaux region, of throwing the crushed grapes into the air with wooden shovels before placing them in the fermenting-vat.

Yeasts are very sensitive, also, to heat and cold. They are capable of existing [1] — though not of reproducing — at extremely low temperatures (−300° F.

---

[1] Yeasts are notoriously long-lived. Pacottet, in 1907, isolated yeast from a bottle of sparkling Saumur 1894; placing it in fresh must, he had strong fermentation within forty-eight hours; in the same year he also isolated yeasts from some Anjou wines of the year 1848, these being in perfect condition.

and lower); they do not show signs of activity unless the temperature is at least 60° F., and they do their best work between 65° and 80° F. As the temperature rises above that point, they become still more active, but beyond 98° F. their rate of reproduction and of the production of alcohol becomes progressively slower, stopping entirely at about 105° F. If this heat is maintained for from forty minutes to an hour or more, they are killed; at still higher temperatures they die more quickly — in ten minutes at 140° F. This should be slightly qualified, however, for different strains of yeasts react differently to variations in temperature. It is even possible to " train " a strain to work at unusually low or high temperatures — a fact of tremendous importance in hot countries such as Southern California. But in general it is nevertheless true that they do their work best at moderate temperatures. In contrast to their temperate habits, the harmful bacteria which induce sickness in the wine are positively tropical in their preferences. Their real activity begins at the temperature in which the *saccharomyces* begin to slow down. Consequently wine-makers exert every effort to keep their must at a temperature which allows the maximum activity of the good yeasts, but discourages the activity of the harmful bacteria — that is, between 70° and 80° F.

The fact has already been mentioned that a must which is high in acidity generally enjoys a better fermentation, because in an acid must the yeasts have a better opportunity to develop. Actually, it makes little difference to the *saccharomyces* whether the must is acid or neutral. *But* the harmful bacteria require a neutral or only barely acid must for their vigorous development. Therefore if the must is sufficiently acid, they are held at bay, and the field is open for the yeasts.

Wine-makers, then, encourage the rapid development of the yeasts in every possible way — by aerating the must, by controlling its temperature, by seeing that it is not deficient in acidity. Many wine-makers go still further and make absolutely sure that the yeasts get a good start by adding vigorous yeast cultures directly as soon as the must is in the vats. These cultures — called *pieds de cuve* in France, *starters* in the United States — are usually made by selecting a small quantity of sound, well-ripened grapes two days in advance, and seeing that they are in full and strong fermentation at the time of the main vintage. A quantity of this actively fermenting mixture, in which the yeasts are multiplying with great vigour, is then added to each vat of fresh must. Another way of preparing starters — the one which is used in most large wineries — is to isolate with the help of a microscope a culture of pure yeast at the end of a successful fermentation and to preserve this dormant culture throughout the year in a refrigerator; just before the vintage this culture is added to a quantity of fresh, pasteurized must, and its rapid development encouraged. A pure culture of this kind eliminates all chance that the bad ferments might develop along with the good in the starter. It also enables the wine-maker to select and perpetuate exactly the strain of yeast which he wants. As a matter of fact, different yeasts are capable of influencing the character of the wine in a considerable degree. The yeasts gathered, for instance, from bananas, apples, or strawberries seem capable of imparting in some degree the aromas of these fruits to whatever liquid they are allowed to ferment. And each viticultural district and variety of grape appears to have an affinity for some one strain of yeast which contributes something to the uniqueness of the wine of that region and that grape. It has been remarked that a strain of yeast may be " trained " to withstand low or high temperature, and it may also be trained to withstand the effects of specific chemicals. The great differences in the behaviour of yeasts led wine-makers to believe at one time that by securing a yeast from some grand vintage they might make a grand wine from the must of inferior grapes. But this supposition did not take into consideration the gross chemical differences between the grapes of the grand vintage and those of the inferior vintage. No one any longer hopes to make a Château Haut-Brion out of Concords.[1]

In large wineries the use of starters is generally joined with some means of inhibiting or destroying the miscellaneous ferments which are present in the

[1] Persons who wish to experiment with various yeasts may buy pure cultures from dealers, but they should secure a reputable dealer. The American Type Culture Collection, which is affiliated with the John McCormick Institute for Infectious Diseases, Chicago, has a great array of yeasts in its vast collection of cultures. Pure cultures of these may be bought quite reasonably. The collection is maintained primarily for the benefit of workers in bacteriological research.

must that is to be started. This is done sometimes by
pasteurizing the must and so killing all ferments, both
good and bad, before adding the starter; but this not
only calls for elaborate equipment and so is very expensive, but has the drawback that the must may be
overheated and thus acquire a *gout de cuit*, or cooked
taste. The other, and more generally practised, method
of impeding the growth of the bad ferments is that
of " sulphuring " the must. The traditional method is
that of burning sulphur in the vat and thus forming
sulphur dioxide. When the must is placed in the vat,
the sulphur dioxide gas is transformed into sulphurous
acid on contact with it; and sulphurous acid has the
property of retarding or destroying the bad ferments
without injuring the good yeasts. It is now more usual
to add sulphurous acid (not to be confused with *sulphuric* acid) or potassium metabisulphite directly to
the must, since it is thus possible to gauge the dose
much more accurately. The French grow lyrical in
their praise of the use of sulphur. Thus M. Chancrin
writes that: " Sulphurous acid invariably (whether
the fruit be healthy or altered) causes a general improvement in the quality of the wine. . . . This improvement, clear enough so far as white wines are
concerned, is also apparent for red wines, notably in
regard to their *colour*, their *taste*, and their *constitution*." It is regarded, in a word, as a sort of universal
panacea for all the humours to which wine is subject.
There can be little doubt, when the fruit is not all
that it should be, that the judicious use of sulphurous
acid can work near-miracles; but when the fruit is

sound and ripe and every condition conspires to a strong and normal fermentation, it is permissible to doubt the need for such dosing.

After the wine-maker has done everything within his power to assure a favourable fermentation, very little time elapses before the must in the vats begins to show definite signs of activity. Within twenty-four hours there is a distinct odour of escaping gas about the open mouth of the vat, and the gentle gurgle is heard. The must begins to heave, like the lava of a restive volcano, and the solid matter of the grapes rises to the surface, forming what the French call the *chapeau*. If a hole is poked through the chapeau, the liquid beneath bubbles and foams. Fermentation is under way. Steadily the fermentation gathers force; the gurgling becomes louder, the frothing more violent, the chapeau more densely packed, the odour of the gas more sharply insistent, so that if it is breathed directly it produces a sharp, choking sensation. In large wineries which do not have forced draft ventilation, there are strict rules against approaching the vats without permission, and people have been suffocated to death by the gas; for it is heavier than air and gradually displaces it. Persons entering a fermenting-cellar when the violent fermentation is under way usually carry a lighted candle, which goes out if the gas is too thick for safety.

The systems of *cuvage* — that is, the actual conduct of the violent fermentation — differ greatly from one wine-making region to another. In many the " open " system is employed, by which the chapeau is allowed to float unimpeded on the surface of the fermenting must. When this method is used, the chapeau is broken up at regular intervals, at least twice a day, and thoroughly mixed with the juice which has separated from it. This is done partly because the yeasts develop more rapidly at the surface and it is desirable to distribute them evenly throughout the whole fermenting mass, and partly to allow all of the liquid an even contact with the skins, which contain the colouring matter; partly also because, if allowed to stay at the surface, some of the colouring matter may become oxidized by exposure to the air and will so be lost to the wine, and partly to hinder the development of acetic fermentation. In Burgundy the wine-makers used to break up the chapeau by stripping off their clothes, climbing onto the solid mass, and gradually working their way down into it, where they thrashed about until they were completely exhausted or could stand the fumes no longer. This method may be, and has been, criticized quite freely on sanitary, æsthetic, and humanitarian grounds, and I do not know that it is still used anywhere. A more general practice where open fermentation is used is to break the chapeau with wooden poles or paddles.

Another commonly used method is that of pushing the chapeau a few inches beneath the surface of the must and holding it there by means of a perforated or grilled wooden lid which fits down inside of the vat and is there secured. The perforations allow the fermenting must to circulate, whilst keeping the solid matter from rising to the top. Still another method is that of splitting the chapeau into layers, each of which is held in place by one of these lids; this is merely a refinement of the one just described. These various systems of cuvage all have their enthusiastic adherents, not to mention their detractors. But that which is perhaps most generally employed is a combination of open and submerged fermentation. Until the fermentation is well under way, it is left open, in order to encourage a strong development of yeasts; when the yeasts are well developed, the chapeau is submerged, and the yeasts, being thus forced to adopt their anaerobic way of life, perform a thorough job of converting the sugar into alcohol.

During the violent fermentation the temperature of the must rises considerably. When the fermentation is being carefully conducted, the frequent taking of the temperature of the must is as much a routine practice as it is in a hospital. If it threatens to rise above the danger point, at which the bad ferments stir to activity, heroic measures are taken to bring the temperature down, by means of coils which surround the vat or are submerged in it and through which a refrigerant is pumped. Another method of coping with the problem of high temperature is based on the fact that yeasts, like human beings, may be anæsthetized with chloroform. If in the course of violent fermentation the temperature of the vat reaches a dangerous point, chloroform is pumped into it, the yeasts pass into a coma, the fermentation ceases, and the temperature of the fermenting mass is thus caused to fall; if the chloroform is later driven off, fermentation may be resumed. However, this method has a number of disadvantages and has no advantages over the method of cooling by coils; consequently it has not been used save experimentally.

Wine-makers who proceed on a less scientific plane devise rough and ready methods of cooling, or simply trust to luck and a prompt turn in the weather. They quickly develop a certain fatalism about such matters.

A sudden drop in temperature, if great enough, can be troublesome to the wine-maker, though it is not nearly so dangerous to the wine as a rise. Wine-makers in cool climates use equipment somewhat similar to that used in hot climates, except that they turn warm water through their coils instead of re-frigerants; or they have facilities for regulating the temperature of their fermenting-cellars.

However, if the fermentation goes forward smoothly, with no such trying interludes, the violence begins presently to subside. The bubbling is reduced to a murmur, and the chapeau, hitherto held up by the force of the gas rising through the must, sinks gradually to the bottom. Wine-makers measure the progress of the fermentation by means of a sac-charometer, the same instrument with which the sugar-content of the must is measured before fermen-tation begins. The saccharometer, which is known also among wine-makers as a " stem " or " spindle," is a very simple and inexpensive little instrument which every wine-maker ought to own. More of it later.

When the fermentation is " normal," the sugar is

transformed into alcohol at the rate of perhaps four per cent a day; so that a must of twenty per cent sugar is fermented out dry in about five days. But the period varies. Sometimes the task is finished in three days of fermentation, sometimes it requires two weeks. Then it is time to think of drawing off and pressing. The precise moment for pressing is as much a matter of individual preference and regional custom as is the type of *cuvage*. In the Bordeaux district the unpressed wine is left on its *marc* [1] sometimes for several weeks after the violent fermentation is finished. The Bordelais have successfully rationalized this traditional practice. Wine-makers in central Europe sometimes leave the wine on the marc all winter, on the theory that it adds " strength " to the wine. The Burgundians, on the other hand, have a saying: the quicker the fermentation, the better the wine; and they make haste to separate the new wine from its marc at the earliest possible opportunity. In the United States the customary practice, both in California and in the Eastern wineries, was to draw down and press when the must still contained a considerable quantity of unfermented sugar. In the Sandusky wineries they used frequently to draw down when the sugar-content was still as high as ten per cent. Like the practice of the Burgundians and that of the Bordelais, this is supposed to have many points in its favour. All three produce good wines.

The object of pressing is to separate the new wine from the gross indissoluble matter which remains after

[1] The solid residue.

fermentation, principally the skins, the stems, and the seeds. Ordinarily the new wine is allowed to drain of its own weight from the marc, and this wine is esteemed the finest of the vintage and sometimes kept separate from the rest. When all has drained that is going to drain, the saturated mass which remains is transferred to the press, and the produce of the first pressing is also sometimes kept separate. The marc, which has been pressed to a compact and apparently quite dry mass, is loosened and stirred about with wood-tined pitchforks or other appropriate implements and given another pressing. Sometimes there is even a third pressing; and the most " progressive " proprietors employ a rather complicated apparatus for extracting the last reluctant drops from the marc which is based on the principle of diffusion. Finally the marc is set aside either for the making of sugar wine or piquette, or for distillation. In some regions the marc fresh from the press is used as fodder for draught animals.[1] Distillation of thoroughly pressed marc yields a very fiery and indelicate liquor, the poor man's cognac. In the more meticulous establishments the drawn wine and that of each pressing are kept separate; and chemical analysis shows, as a matter of fact, that the products of these pressings vary considerably. The press wines are much richer in tannin and possess a higher acidity, and are consequently much greener and slower to mature. Save in the mak-

[1] Says Fabre: " *L'alcool qu'ils renferment leur communique de légères propriétés excitants, éminemment favorables aux efforts pénibles qu'on exige de ces animaux.*"

ing of fine wines, however, the press wines are customarily blended with the drawn wines.

After the pressing the new wine is transferred to the casks or other containers in which, during the gentle secondary fermentation, all remaining traces of sugar are eliminated and the wine undergoes the many subtle and deliberate changes which transform it from a liquid which is merely alcoholic into something which richly rewards the patience and care which have been lavished upon it.

Chapter Five

RED WINE

THE AMERICAN wine-maker has two great classes of
wine grapes to choose from: the varieties of *Vitis
vinifera* which are grown in California and to a very
limited extent in Texas, New Mexico, Arizona, and
Utah, and the varieties which have been developed
from our native species and are grown, for the most
part, east of the Rocky Mountains.

CALIFORNIA RED-WINE VARIETIES

Comparatively few of the red-wine varieties are
shipped in large quantities from California to the
Eastern markets, because the demand for the choicest
of them is not sufficiently great to warrant the effort,
and also because certain varieties (usually, alas! the
less choice) withstand the long ride more successfully
than the rest. Wine-makers who live on the Pacific
Coast are therefore fortunate in having a much larger
assortment, of their own growing and in the markets.
Most of the red-wine varieties ripen during late September and early October. Long before that the amateur wine-maker has begun to glance daily at the

[132

produce reports which appear in every newspaper
and which record the arrival of the first grapes in the
market. Around the middle of September he makes
his first visit to the wholesale produce district, to have
a preliminary reconnoitre, or, if he is an old hand, to
renew acquaintance with the produce dealers. These
are mostly Italians, and very pleasant fellows they
are, anxious to fill the unwary with the most extravagant misinformation and not at all disturbed if they
are exposed. They are also willing to bargain. The
California grapes are shipped in flat boxes, called
" lugs," which contain from twenty-two to twenty-
six pounds apiece. These stand on display along the
curbings in great stacks, and the shipments keep coming in all through October and well into November.
The prime crop usually arrives during the first two
weeks of October. A " lug " may be counted upon to
yield between a gallon and a gallon and a half of
finished wine.

The varieties which appear most frequently in the
Eastern markets are the following:

Alicante Bouschet. This grape, which is always to
be found in the Eastern markets, is the most largely
grown of all the California red-wine types. Its sugar-
content and its acidity are both ideal for the making
of a table wine of medium body. The wine has a very
intense deep garnet-red colour, though the pigment
tends to precipitate rather rapidly. It is used a good
deal for blending with other wines to secure a wine
of the " Burgundy " type. The grape has an interesting history. It is one of several hybrids which were

made by Henri Bouschet in 1865 between the Alicante, a very productive vine that is much grown in southern Europe and forms the basis of most of the ordinary Spanish red wines, and the Teinturier, which is grown chiefly for its colour. It has proved to be the most successful hybrid ever deliberately made and is grown to vast acreage in every *vinifera*-producing region of the world. The bunches are large and rather loose, the berries also large and covered with a deep bloom. The skin is thick, and the grapes stand shipment better than any other variety. The full correct name of this grape is Alicante-Henri Bouschet; it is usually shipped merely as Alicante.

Carignane. The Carignane, which the produce dealers always pronounce Carrigan, also comes into the Eastern markets in large quantities. Its sugar-content averages twenty-two per cent, which is ideal for a dry red wine, and it is rich in acidity. This latter quality gives the young wine a harshness that is not particularly agreeable; but with aging it wears off and a pleasant bouquet develops. It has plenty of colour. This is a grape of great antiquity, if not of noble lineage. It is of Spanish origin, being still grown largely around Cariñena, and its history has been traced back as far as the twelfth century. It is now also grown a great deal in southern France, in Algeria, and on the Cape. Its bunches are large and compact, and its berries, which are black, have a thick bloom. The skin is thick, so that it travels well.

Grenache. This grape, which is also of Spanish

origin, yields a wine which much resembles that of the Carignane, though its sugar-content is apt to run somewhat higher, and its colour is somewhat lighter. It is the basis, in Europe, of some very good wines, and also of some very bad ones. When grown in southern California, its sugar-content is frequently too high for the making of a dry wine; it is then used for sweet red wines and for angelica. It does not do well in the California Coast counties, where the best dry-wine grapes are grown. In appearance it is much like the Carignane.

Mataro. The Mataro is often confused with the Grenache and the Carignane. Its sugar-content is high, but seldom too high for the making of a dry wine, and its colour is excellent. It has a rather high acidity. Before prohibition many of the best wines of Napa and Sonoma counties and of Santa Clara were the product of the Mataro. It is still another grape of Spanish origin, and it is still very popular in Spain. In the sixteenth century it was imported from there into southern France, where it is still a fairly important grape, and was brought to California in the seventies of the nineteenth century. It ships well, but because of the compactness of its bunches it sometimes develops mould.

Mission. The history of this grape, which was the first *vinifera* to be grown in California, was discussed pretty thoroughly in Chapter iii. It is now seen much less than it used to be, since it has been replaced by better varieties. The sugar-content is high, and it is consequently used mostly in the production of sweet wines. Although it is a " black " grape, its colour is notoriously weak.

Petite Sirah. Of the grapes which make a fairly frequent appearance in the Eastern markets, this is by far the best. Its sugar-content runs about twenty-two per cent, and its acidity is normal; the grape itself has no characteristic flavour, and its prominent seeds and tough skin make it worthless for eating. But the wine! Its robe of purple delights the eye, and the subsequent degustation bears out the promise of its rich colour. The Petite Sirah of France predominates in the best vignobles of the Rhone valley, and there it is known variously as Schiras, Shiraz, Syrah, Sirah, Syrac, Sirac, and Marsanne; and there are some who say that it is the same as the Barbera, which flourishes over the border in nothern Italy. Strangely enough, the grape which we call Petite Sirah — which is both grown and marketed under that name — has turned out not to be the true Petite Sirah at all. Bioletti says of it: " When the Petite Sirah was introduced into California, its bearing was disappointing. Certain vines in the plantations, however, were noted as good bearers. These were selected as the source of cuttings for new vineyards, and finally good yielding vineyards were obtained. This has been used . . . as an illustration of the improvement of a variety by selection on the basis of ' performance records.' Unfortunately for the theory it has been found that the Petite Sirah was not improved but eliminated. All that was done was to select cuttings from another variety of similar appearance which had been mixed with the Sirah. This variety is the Duriff and is well known in France, where it is grown in the same district as the Sirah." Consequently, though those who buy Sirah may expect an excellent wine, they will be unwise to look for a Châteauneuf-du-Pape or an Hermitage.

Zinfandel. In Zinfandel we have probably the most famous of all the California red-wine varieties. It was one of the first of the *vinifera* to be introduced into California during the mid-century grape boom, and because of its qualities as a prolific grower and the excellent character of its wine it quickly overtook the Mission in popularity. Its wine has a very characteristic flavour, and before prohibition it was much used by the shippers of the better bottled dry wines, either straight or in blend with wines of deeper colour. It is undoubtedly of Hungarian origin. The bunch is large and compact, and the berries medium in size and black, with a blue bloom. Since the skin is thin, it does not ship as well as many other varieties; but it is sent east in large quantities none the less, largely because of its popularity among the Italo-Americans. They usually blend it with an equal quantity of Alicante.

The seven varieties described above are those most commonly found in the Eastern markets. All of them produce excellent dry red wines, though in no sense " fine " wines. In the following list are varieties which appear in the markets only sporadically, but which may sometimes be secured by arrangement with a friendly fruit-dealer who plans to order a car-load of the scarcer varieties for his own use or that of his friends. Persons who live on the Pacific Coast will of course find it much easier to get these varieties:

Barbera. See Petite Sirah. The vine was imported independently from Italy, and is grown under its own name. Its wine is slow to mature, but worth the waiting.

Crabb's Black Burgundy. Bonnet says of this grape: "Variety identical with the variety known as Refosco. . . . The bunches are conical, loose to well filled. The berries are medium, spherical, black, and of a medium juicy texture. The variety is grown especially in northern Coast counties of California. . . . As to intrinsic qualities it suffices to say that this variety used to give some of the best wines produced in the Coast counties. It has deep color." Its qualities as wine much more resemble clarets than Burgundies. Hilgard called this " probably the most mischievous of the misnomers of California nomenclature.

Cabernet. There are two subvarieties of this grape: Cabernet Sauvignon and Cabernet Franc. They were brought to California from the Gironde, where they form the basis of the very finest vintage clarets. They constitute the entire growth of Château Lafite, for instance. Unfortunately they produce reluctantly, their yield per acre being much less than half that of such prolific vines as Alicante Bouschet. There is only one epithet for the wine-maker who passes up an opportunity to get some Cabernet. The grape is very unprepossessing in appearance, being small and covered with brown spots.

Freisa. The special strawberry-like bouquet of

Freisa is very much esteemed, especially by the Italians. It is a vine of Italian origin, being much grown in the Piedmont.

Grignolino. Another vine of Italian origin, grown in California largely by the Italians. During the past few years a good deal of Grignolino has been transformed into concentrate, in which form it is occasionally to be found in Italian delicatessen stores.

Malbec. A minor vine of the Bordeaux region. Not much of it is grown.

Merlot. This vine is also grown a good deal in the Bordeaux region of France. In Bordeaux the proprietors of the lesser growths find it expedient to blend a little of the Cabernet with more productive and less capricious growths, of which Merlot is one. Thus they impart the Cabernet flavour to a much larger quantity of wine. It is in no way comparable to the Cabernet. It is not very much grown in California.

Pinot Noir. The Pinot has been the great informing vine of the Burgundian wines as far back as the fame of those wines extends. The name of Pinot is almost a guarantee of a fine wine, and the great vintage Burgundies are made of it alone. Like the noble Cabernet, this vine is a poor producer; like the Cabernet it is worth the effort. Its great age has given it many diminutive and regional names, of which some are: Noirien, Franc Pineau, Petit Verot, Auvernat Noir, Plant Noble, Orleans, Rouget, Pinot Burgunder, Vert Doré, Plant Médaillé, Morillon Noir, Petit Bourguignon, Czerna Okrudla Ranka, Blauer Burgunder, Schwertzkleuner, and so on. (Incidentally, this multiplication of names, which is a characteristic of most good and rewarding varieties, is a source of endless confusion. One is always finding that a grape is not what one thought it was, or that it is what one didn't think it was.)

Saint Macaire. Still another of the grapes which are grown around Bordeaux for blending with Cabernet.

NATIVE RED-WINE GRAPES

The Concord has so crowded out the better varieties of native red-wine grapes that they are very hard to find in the markets. Since prohibition they have been cultivated less and less for market, because the amateur has had no means of knowing their virtues. A selection of the best varieties is here included for a number of reasons: first, they do occasionally get into the markets; second, it is often possible, if one has sufficient interest, to track down some of them by scouting around the country-side and inquiring when a vineyard is spotted. The farmers are invariably glad to discuss their grapes, the more so if they cling stubbornly to an unappreciated variety, and are even happier to sell them. Since few persons know the best native wine varieties from those which are unfit for wine-making, and since few of them are much good for anything else, it is generally possible to buy them quite reasonably. One fruit farmer near Baltimore pulled up a vineyard of Nortons two years ago because no one would buy them. A third reason for including this list is that some of these varieties do well in almost every part of the country and may be

[140

planted and tended with no little pleasure and profit. Any reliable nurseryman will quote prices. Enough first-quality one-year plants may be bought for five dollars to yield a bountiful home vintage.[1]

The Eastern varieties begin to mature late in September and appear in the markets most plentifully during October. They are sold either in twelve-quart Climax baskets or in half-bushel baskets. Local crops are sometimes sold by the bushel. Native grapes and California grapes are seldom handled by the same dealer.

Bacchus. The parents of this grape are the wild *V. riparia,* a native species which has sired several good red-wine grapes, and *V. labrusca.* Its sugar-content runs around nineteen per cent, and its acidity is always high. It is grown a good deal in northern Ohio and a little in New York State. Its flavour is good, and its colour excellent.

Clevener. This grape, which is a hybrid of *V. riparia* and *V. labrusca,* is still grown considerably in the wine-making region which centres in Egg Harbor, New Jersey. It was also grown a good deal, for its red wine, in the Finger Lake wine region of New York State.

Clinton. This is one of the first of the native hybrids to be used on any considerable scale for wine-making, having been known as early as 1815. It did not acquire its present name until a good many years later. It is probably the first of the recognized *riparia* hybrids,

[1] See Appendix. The map indicates what varieties will grow where.

and it has been the parent of many others. Like so many of our native wine grapes, and all of the *riparia* varieties, it is unfit for consumption " out of hand " because of its high acidity, but its wine, though harsh when young, is much esteemed.

Cynthiana. See Norton.

Eumelan. This grape, which used to be a very popular native wine grape, has the blood of three species, *labrusca, vinifera,* and *æstivalis,* in its vines. It was not only very popular as a red-wine grape, but was much used in blending for sparkling white wines.

Flowers. This is one of the best of the black Muscadines, which are indigenous to Virginia and the Carolinas. Its colour and its aroma are almost unbelievably intense. Its sugar is apt to be quite low and its acidity quite high. The Southerners make from it a dark and syrupy, and faintly nauseating, tipple, by the addition of much sugar. A little of this goes a long way.

Herbemont. This is a pure seedling of *V. bourquiniana* and is grown considerably in the South. It is, for the United States, an ancient variety; Hedrick says that it has been traced back to before the Revolution, though its name was received many years later. It was imported in great quantity with Lenoir into France at the height of the phylloxera epidemic. The quality of its fruit, when grown on the French calcareous soils, was inferior; and the French today hold no love for it. Munson used this grape as a basis for many of the hybrids which he produced in Texas.

Ives. This is still another *riparia* hybrid, and it used to be the basis of many very good Eastern red wines.

[142

It was grown a good deal around Cincinnati at one time and was later cultivated extensively on the island vineyards of Lake Erie. It is still grown in the Egg Harbor district.

James. This grape is another of the black Muscadines. The Southerners treat it as they do the Flowers.

Lenoir. This is probably the best-known of all the cultivated varieties of *V. bourquiniana.* During the phylloxera scare it was imported into France in great quantity both as a direct producer and as a root-stock for grafting. Its cultivation is confined to the Southern states (it is nothing like the Southern Muscadines, however), where it has always been much used for wine. Its wine is a deep ruby-red.

Norton. Most Eastern wine-makers consider Norton the best of the native red-wine grapes. It is a cultivated variety of the species *V. æstivalis,* the wild Chicken grape of the east central states. Norton is so much like Cynthiana that they cannot be told apart; in a word, they are the same. Norton has always been grown in all of the important Eastern wine districts and was particularly successful in Missouri.

The list of native wine types might be greatly extended, but there is little use in doing it, for the grapes are not grown on any considerable scale. Many of the varieties, indeed, would have died out long since had it not been for enlightened amateurs who still cling to them. The low estate of these grapes is very discouraging.

THE QUESTION OF EQUIPMENT

It will be assumed for the purpose of exposition that approximately twenty gallons of red wine are to be made, from some one of the more accessible California varieties, such as Alicante Bouschet or Zinfandel. The person who proposes to make wine for his own use may make it in smaller quantities if he chooses; but five gallons require almost as much work as twenty, and if he has moderate success, he will very soon be regretting that he did not make more. It is surprising how little time is needed to do away with twenty gallons of a sound dry red wine. Indeed, the foresighted wine-maker will ferment several batches of twenty gallons apiece, from different varieties, for some of it thus has a better chance to reach a full maturity before it is used up. The commonest error of the amateur wine-maker is to begin his operations on so small a scale that he is not able to get ahead of the demands of immediate consumption. Thus his wine never has a chance to mature properly.

The following equipment is recommended:

Pails. Two pails are necessary. They should be of ten- or twelve-quart size, and they should be enamelled or heavily tinned. The enamelled type is preferable. They may be bought in the basement of any department store.

Crusher. The grapes may be crushed by foot-power in the bathtub, but the method is not recommended. Better to buy, or borrow, a hopper-type crusher, which will do in a few minutes what is accomplished by five miles of prancing in a bathtub. The crusher may be bought at any bottler's supply-house for around five dollars, and there are two great species: the single-roller type, with galvanized metal hopper and heavily tinned roller; the double-roller type, with wooden hopper. The latter is preferable, since the two meshed rollers are so designed that seeds cannot possibly be crushed between them; however, the single-hopper type is quite satisfactory. The best size is one with a hopper about twenty-four inches square, as this holds just one " lug " of grapes.

Fermenting-vat. The best vat for the small-scale wine-maker is a fifty-gallon white oak barrel set on end with the top head removed. The head is easily removed by knocking off the two top hoops with a hammer and a cold-chisel or old screw-driver, pounding the head into the barrel with hammer or mallet, then pulling it out edgewise and replacing the hoops. The hoops should be driven home tight. Save the head of the barrel; it will be useful. The barrel should be white oak, *not red oak*, and it should be of the waxed type, not charred.[1] One should be very leery about buying a second-hand barrel, making sure that it has held nothing the odour or taste of which will reappear later in the wine. Before it is used, the vat should be half-filled with clean water and left standing for twenty-four hours, then rinsed thoroughly with a hose. The French often swabbed vats with a little

[1] Barrels are supplied waxed, charred, or plain. A fifty-gallon barrel costs between four and five dollars and may be bought from a cooper, a mail-order house, or any malt shop.

brandy or grain alcohol. After it has been used, the vat requires slightly more elaborate treatment for subsequent fermentations. It is soaked for half a day, then scrubbed out thoroughly with a hot solution of washing soda and rinsed with a hose; after it has dried for half a day, a coat of new paraffin is applied to its interior, and it is ready. (The paraffin, of the type used on jelly and sold in every grocery store, is melted in a saucepan and quickly slapped on with a clean dry paint-brush.)

If one proposes to keep the drawn wine and the press wine separate (this is hardly worth while when only twenty gallons are made), a 1½-inch hole is drilled in the side of the barrel-vat about five inches above the bottom, and a wooden spigot is driven in with a mallet. The spigot hole ought to be drilled in the centre of the widest barrel stave.

Before it is filled, the vat should be mounted on a small stand or table about eighteen inches high. This stand should be sturdy, for a barrel full of must is not light. The stand is absolutely necessary if one proposes to draw down; otherwise it is impossible to get a pail beneath the spigot.

Press. The wine may be pressed by hand, of course, like jelly in cloth bags; but this is very laborious and the pressing is not thorough. The type of press that is illustrated on page 147 is quite satisfactory; it may be bought at any bottler's supply-house or from a mail-order house, or (usually) from a hardware store. A borrowed cider-press is perfectly satisfactory. It is unwise to buy too small a press, of the kind that is put on a table, since sufficient pressure cannot be obtained with it, and it extends the process of pressing needlessly. The diameter of the press illustrated is sixteen

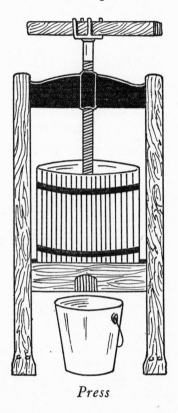

Press

inches, and it is sixteen inches deep. The pressing cage comes apart for thorough cleaning. In buying a press it is very important to see that the uprights are true, that the press bed is substantially mounted, and that the screw and screw-casting are; otherwise it will be subjected to terrific stresses and its life will be short.

Bags. Two substantial cloth bags are needed for pressing. It is important that these bags be very strong and also porous. Burlap bags are satisfactory. " Monk's cloth," which may be bought in the drapery department of any department store, is much better. It is both strong and porous. The bags should be about twenty inches wide at the mouth and twenty-five inches deep, and the seams should be on the sides, not across the bottom, as that is where most of the strain comes; the seams should be sewed double, then turned and sewed two or three times more, with stout thread.

Funnel. A large enamelled funnel is necessary. The mouth of the funnel should be about one inch in diameter, so that it will not clog.

Tub. An old-fashioned wooden laundry-tub, or a large enamelled baby's bathtub, or a couple of large dishpans, are useful to hold the marc after the wine is pressed from it. There is no need to buy a special container for this purpose.

Saccharometer. The saccharometer, or sugar meter, is all but indispensable. It is merely a hollow, sealed tube of glass about a foot long, weighted at one end so that it floats upright in a liquid, and marked along its length with a scale from which one reads directly the percentage of sugar in the solution. It works on the specific-gravity principle; that is, it takes advantage of the fact that a solution of sugar is heavier than plain water and thus causes a floating object of given weight to ride higher in it. When the saccharometer is placed

in water, it sinks to the o which is marked on its side.
If the solution is twenty-two per cent sugar, it sinks

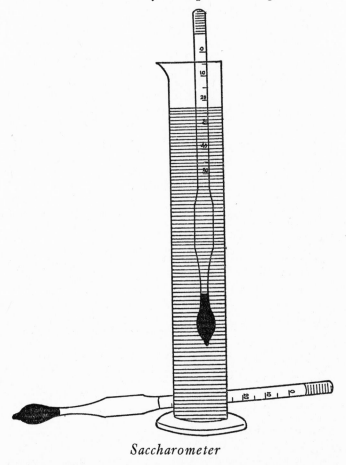

Saccharometer

only to the point marked 22. There are several saccharometer scales, of which Brix or Balling are those

usually found. They measure sugar-content directly in percentage by weight. The British, with their passion for individuality, measure the density of sugar-solutions in a special unit, known as the *degree Twaddle;* by all means avoid a saccharometer scaled in degrees Twaddle. An ordinary Brix or Balling saccharometer may be bought at any laboratory supply-house and from many opticians for from fifty cents to two dollars. The scales are accurate at 60° F., and progressively inaccurate as that norm is departed from (though any temperature between 55° and 75° gives a reading sufficiently accurate for practical purposes). More accurate saccharometers, which contain a thermometer that automatically corrects for variations in temperature, are made,[1] but they are not really necessary.

With the saccharometer one should buy a plain hydrometer jar, of glass, about fifteen inches long and two or two and a half inches in diameter, which costs fifty cents. It is also wise to get a small floating thermometer. This may be bought in any pet-store (they are widely used for measuring the temperature of fish-bowls and babies' baths) and also in some of the more enlightened ten-cent stores.

Burette. This is used in measuring acidity. It is not absolutely necessary. Its use will be described presently. It may be bought from a laboratory supply-house for a dollar and a half.

Containers for the Wine. It is very important to have proper containers for the new wine; it is in these

[1] By the Taylor Instrument Companies, Rochester, among others.

that they spend the greater part of their life, and the wrong containers may easily injure their health or even doom them to a miserable death. Traditionally, wines are kept in wood, which means white oak casks, thoroughly clean and sweet. Traditionalists maintain that the secondary fermentation and the aging of wine cannot be carried out satisfactorily in anything else, that the " breathing " which takes place through the pores of the wood plays an important part in the aging of wine. But for the small wine-maker they have the disadvantage that they allow a considerable proportion of the wine to evaporate (the smaller the cask, the greater, proportionately, the area of its walls; consequently the larger the proportion of wine that evaporates); they must therefore be replenished constantly with more wine, and the small wine-maker sometimes finds himself without any wine with which to replenish.

Five-gallon glass bottles have been found to be far more satisfactory when the quantity is not large. These were used a great deal in commercial wineries when wine was being made experimentally in small quantities, and during prohibition home wine-makers have been largely won over to them. Their advantages are many. They are easy to handle, filled or empty (and this is no small consideration when wine-making is being conducted in a small house or apartment). They are very easy to clean. It is possible at all times to see the state of the wine's development — whether it is clearing, whether it is turgid, whether it is making a steady precipitation of the lees, etc. Finally, since there is no breathing through their sides, there is no loss by evaporation. Five five-gallon bottles are needed in making twenty gallons of wine; they may be bought for about seventy-five cents apiece from bottling supply-houses, and second-hand for somewhat less. It is also a good idea to have several one-gallon and perhaps a two-gallon bottle for odd quantities. The larger ten- or twelve-gallon carboys are not recommended; they are fragile and unevenly blown and apt to crack when washed.

Miscellaneous. A ⅝-inch red rubber hose for siphoning, six feet long. A roll of absorbent cotton. Clean cloths for wiping.

That is the list of necessary equipment. It will seem fairly long to the novice, but almost everything is permanent equipment, and it is often possible to borrow a press or crusher or pails or baby's bathtub from a friend, thus spreading the capital expenditure over several vintages. Another solution of the first-cost problem is to share capital expense with a friend. But it should be remembered that even though expenses for equipment are figured in, the cost of the wine is very low.

HOW TO PROCEED

Wine-making is best done in a room that is given over to the purpose, which has a concrete floor with a drain and plenty of hot and cold running water and is not subject to excessive fluctuations of temperature. Ideally, its temperature should be controllable. Actually, when done at home, wine-making proceeds more often than not by a series of compromises as to space and location; the fermenting-room is more than apt to be the laundry or a corner of the kitchen, the *cave* a corner of the basement between the coal-bin and the work-bench.

If twenty gallons of wine are to be made, sixteen "lugs" of grapes are the correct quantity. Grapes vary considerably in their juiciness, but this is close enough. More is apt to crowd a fifty-gallon vat. Once the grapes have been bought, or gathered, it is best to proceed with the vinification at once.

Crushing. The fermenting-vat or barrel must be thoroughly clean. The crusher must be washed with hot water and washing soda and then thoroughly rinsed. The crusher is placed directly across the open top of the vat, which has been put on its little stand or table.

Pick over the grapes and eliminate badly mouldered bunches, if there are any, throwing the sound grapes directly in the hopper of the crusher. It is not necessary to inspect each berry; it is not necessary to worry if some of them have started to become raisins or if some of the berries have split. The grapes should not be washed. When the hopper is full, turn the crank of the crusher, and the crushed bunches, dripping juice, plop directly into the vat.

One of the long-standing controversies among wine-makers is whether the grapes should be stemmed or not (the practice is called *égrappage* in France). The grape stems are rich in tannin, and tannin is of course necessary to wine. However, tannin is also supplied by seeds and skins, and some œnologists maintain that the removal of the stems, which cuts

Crusher Mounted on Fermenting Vat

down the quantity of tannin somewhat, relieves the new wine of much of its harshness and allows it to mature more rapidly. There is undoubtedly much

[154

truth in this, and stemming is practised in many of the finest wine-making regions. It is generally practised in California. Opponents contend that the stems, because of their bulk, help to aerate the mass and thus promote a stronger fermentation, and that the additional tannin helps to bring out the colour. A good compromise is to remove half of the stems. Good wines are made both with and without the stems.

The vat should not be filled more than three-fourths full of crushed grapes. Sixteen " lugs " fill a fifty-gallon barrel just about three-fourths full.

The crusher should be thoroughly rinsed as soon as the crushing is over, before the juice dries on it.

ANALYSING AND CORRECTING THE MUST

The must, composed of the crushed bunches of grapes, is now in the fermenting-vat. It should be analysed and, if necessary, corrected. Practically speaking, the only two important tests are those for *sugar-content* and for *acidity*. All wine-makers test for sugar; the test for acidity is not absolutely necessary and few amateur wine-makers bother with it.

Testing for Sugar. There are several ways of testing for sugar, but for practical purposes there is no need for measurement more accurate than that by means of the saccharometer. With a clean glass tumbler dip some of the fresh juice from the must in the vat and strain this juice through several layers of clean cheese-cloth into the hydrometer jar. Set the jar on a level table. Insert the floating thermometer and take the temperature of the juice. If it falls within 55° and

75° F., well and good; if it is higher, pop it into the ice-box for a few minutes. Insert the saccharometer, and when it is floating quite free and still, take the reading at the surface of the liquid. Do *not* take the reading at the top of the meniscus which forms around

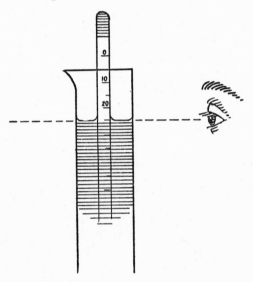

Reading the Saccharometer

the spindle, but at the bottom — that is, at the *true* surface of the liquid.

Correcting Sugar-content. Normally the sugar-content of the juice [1] will fall between 18 and 25 per cent. If the grapes are not fully ripe, the proportion of sugar will fall below 18 per cent; if the grapes are over-ripe, they may occasionally exceed 25 per cent.

[1] Of those varieties listed on pages 132–43.

Some varieties, of course, regularly exceed 25 per cent, but they are not dry-wine grapes.

If the grapes have less than 18 per cent sugar, their wine is thin, sour, and unstable, and their juice must be brought up to standard if drinkable wine is to be made from them. If the grapes have more than 25 per cent, the fermentation is often irregular, proceeding by a series of fits and starts, and there is a danger that it may never be complete and that some of the sugar may remain in the finished wine, to cause trouble later. It is therefore necessary to bring the sugar content to a norm — 22 per cent — by adding sugar or by adding water, as the case may be.

A deficiency of sugar is made up by the addition of ordinary granulated sugar (sucrose). It was formerly thought that grape sugar should be used; that is a mistake, first, because grape sugar is generally impure, and, second, because it is unnecessary. The sucrose is hydrolized immediately upon solution in the must into grape sugar (dextrose and levulose), which is indistinguishable from that occurring naturally in the grapes. The addition of sugar is strictly regulated by law and confined within narrow limits in all enlightened wine-making countries, but it is allowed and even encouraged when the grapes do not have sufficient sugar of their own to give a satisfactory fermentation. If the must has naturally between 20 and 25 per cent of sugar, there is no need to correct it.

In correcting red-wine must it is impossible to estimate the dose exactly, since it is impossible to know exactly how much of the must is juice and how much solid matter. However, we may assume that your sixteen lugs will yield approximately twenty gallons of juice. The amount of sugar to be added is computed in accordance with the Sugar Table on page 159. Example: Suppose the saccharometer indicates only 10 per cent of sugar in the must. How much sugar per gallon has to be added to bring the must up to 22 per cent? According to the table, 15.3 oz. per gallon must be added. If 20 gallons are being made, add 20 x 15.3 = 306 oz., or 19 pounds.

The sugar should be dissolved in a small quantity of the juice drawn from the vat specially for the purpose and warmed slightly. The dissolved sugar is then added to the vat and stirred thoroughly, in order that it be evenly distributed. The stirring may be done with a clean wooden paddle or with well-washed arms. Since the dose is not exact, the must should be tested again with the saccharometer after the sugar has been thoroughly mixed, in order to make sure that it now falls within the safe limits of sugar-content.

When the must is too sweet, it must be brought to normality by the addition of water — a dubious process at best, and strictly forbidden in all nations where wine-making is subject to regulation. Fortunately the must is seldom too sweet if the proper grapes are used. The way to add water to the must is simply to add it, out of the faucet. The amount to add of course can only be computed roughly, on the assumption that the vat will yield twenty gallons of wine. It should be computed in accordance with the Sugar Table. After

Sugar Table

(For use in bringing the sugar-content of must to a
"normal" of 22 per cent)

Per cent sugar in must	Corresponding weight of sugar in 1 gal. must in oz.	Sugar required to bring 1 gal. to 22% in oz.	Per cent sugar in must	Corresponding weight of sugar in 1 gal. must in oz.	Water required to bring 1 gal. of must to 22% in oz.
8	10.2	17.9	23	29.4	5.8
9	11.5	16.6	24	30.7	11.6
10	12.8	15.3	25	32.	17.4
11	14.	14.	26	33.2	23.2
12	15.3	12.8	27	34.5	29.
13	16.6	11.5	28	35.8	34.8
14	17.9	10.2	29	37.1	40.6
15	19.2	8.9	30	38.4	46.4
16	20.4	7.6	31	39.6	52.2
17	21.7	6.4	32	40.9	58.1
18	23.	5.1	33	42.2	63.9
19	24.3	3.8	34	43.5	69.7
20	25.6	2.5	35	44.8	75.5
21	26.8	1.2	36	46.	81.3
22	28.1	0.			

Note: The table indicates the amount of sugar or water to be
added to *one gallon* of must. The amounts are approximations only.
In measuring sugar or water it is sufficiently accurate to compute on
a "pint's-a-pound" basis.

the water is added, the must should be tested once
more with the saccharometer.

Determining Acidity. Most grapes are sufficiently
acid, and most amateur wine-makers are content to

test for sugar-content alone, taking a chance (and it is not a very long one) that the acidity is satisfactory. But the test for acidity, once the idea is grasped, is so simple that it can be done in a moment or two even though the wine-maker knows little of chemistry.

The total acidity of must or wine is always expressed in terms of an acid of known strength, tartaric acid in the case of must, and sulphuric acid in the case of wine. That is, one says that a given must has a total acidity of 9 grammes per litre expressed in tartaric or 5.85 grammes per litre expressed in sulphuric. Whether one expresses it in tartaric or sulphuric is merely a matter of convenience, for the two expressions may be interchanged by recourse to the fact that one gramme of sulphuric acid is equivalent, as acid, to 1.53 grammes of tartaric. They are converted from one to the other as follows:

grammes tartaric   x   .65 = grammes sulphuric
grammes sulphuric x 1.53 = grammes tartaric

The simplest and surest method of determining the acidity — the method recommended by the chemists of the Department of Agriculture — is that of titration, which, as everyone knows who has studied any chemistry, is simply the neutralization of an acid by a measured quantity of an alkaline solution of known strength. The following method of titrating wine must departs slightly from that recommended by the Department of Agriculture; it is not quite so accurate, but it is easier.

Procedure. The apparatus consists of a *burette* graduated in cubic centimetres and tenths; a *pipette* which holds ten cubic centimetres; some slips of blue

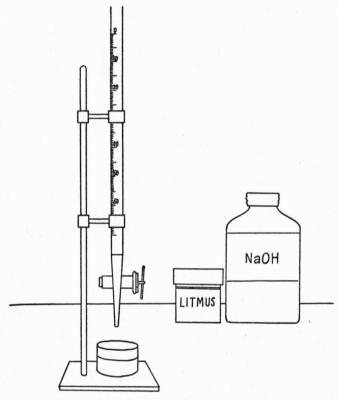

Burette for Use in Testing Acidity

and red *litmus paper*; a small *glass rod*, like that in the top of an iodine bottle; and a clean *cup* or sauce-dish. The burette and pipette may be bought at a laboratory supply-store for very little; the litmus paper for a few cents at any good drug store.

Have a reliable pharmacist make up a litre [1] of *sodium hydroxide* (NaOH) of such strength that one litre exactly neutralizes ten grammes of sulphuric acid. A litre (1 litre = 1,000 c.c.) of this, in other words, corresponds exactly to ten grammes of sulphuric acid; and, of course, 1 c.c. of the solution corresponds to .01 grammes of sulphuric acid.

With the pipette, measure and place in the cup 10 c.c. of the must which is to be tested. Fill the burette with sodium hydroxide solution, up to the point marked 0.

Turn a little of the alkaline solution from the burette into the must and stir with the glass rod. After each addition of the alkaline solution, touch the red and the blue litmus paper with the damp rod. As long as the drop of liquid on the blue paper causes it to turn red, and the red paper shows no change of colour, the must is still acid. Continue to add the sodium hydroxide solution to the must until the damp rod fails to turn the blue paper red, and just barely tinges the red paper with blue. The acid of the must has then been exactly neutralized. If the red paper turns violently blue, then too much of the alkaline solution has been added to the must. The accuracy of the test depends entirely upon titrating exactly to neutrality.

Let us suppose that 8.5 c.c. of the alkaline solution were required to neutralize the acid in the must. Since 1 c.c. of this corresponds to .01 gr. sulphuric acid, the

---

[1] A litre is enough for several dozen tests.

8.5 c.c. correspond to 8.5 c.c. x .01 = .085 gr. of sulphuric acid. The test was made on 10 c.c. of the must: consequently the acidity of 1 litre is .085 gr. x 100 = 8.5 gr. expressed in sulphuric acid. In a word, *with an alkaline solution of the strength here used, all that is necessary is to read directly from the burette the number of cubic centimetres used in order to know the acidity of the must in grammes.* The amount of alkaline solution required was 8.5 c.c.: the acidity of the must is 8.5 gr. per litre expressed in sulphuric acid.

It is simple, as we have seen, to convert acidity from sulphuric to tartaric: 8.5 gr. x 1.53 = 13 gr. per litre expressed in tartaric.

Correcting Acidity. The acidity of American grapes varies from 4 to 18 grammes per litre (as tartaric).[1] The acidity of California varieties does not run that high. Œnologists agree that good wine grapes ought to have an acidity of at least 8 gr. per litre, and on the other hand that an acidity of more than 13 gr. per litre will produce a rather harsh or green wine.

Practically, an excessive amount of acid need cause no apprehension and requires no correction. The excess of acid disappears as the wine ages, precipitating as cream of tartar, and the harshness of the wine is thus tempered by time alone; or else the harshness may be mitigated by blending the wine with another which lacks acidity.

If the must is deficient in acid, however, it is the part of caution to correct the deficiency. " Plastering,"

---

[1] Alwood: *The Chemical Composition of American Grapes.* U. S. Department of Agriculture. Bulletins 145 and 452.

which is merely the addition of a liberal quantity of pure, white plaster of Paris ($Ca SO_4$) at the time of crushing, is the traditional method of increasing the acidity and has been practised in the Mediterranean countries for centuries. But it is now forbidden, or at least closely regulated, in all wine-making countries. It is unsatisfactory, first, because it adds a number of undesirable ingredients to the wine, and, second, because the dose cannot be closely measured. A far better way to increase the acidity is to add a dose of pure tartaric acid to the must in a quantity sufficient to make up for the natural deficiency.

For example: Suppose that our barrel of must shows an acidity of 6 gr. per litre (as tartaric). The barrel is expected to yield approximately 20 gallons of wine: 20 gal. = 75.6 litres.[1] To bring the must to " normal " acidity, add 2 gr. of pure tartaric acid per litre, or a total of 151 gr. The tartaric acid should be dissolved in a small quantity of warm water, added to the must, and thoroughly mixed. The dissolving should be done in a porcelain, glass, or enamelled dish, as the acid attacks metals.

When the acidity of the must is corrected by the addition of pure tartaric acid, no substance is added which does not occur in the must naturally.

Finally, it is a useful rule to remember that *grapes low in sugar are usually high in acidity, and grapes high in sugar are apt to be low in acidity*.

[1] I gal. = 3.78 litres.

RED WINE

FERMENTATION

Let us assume that the fermenting-vat is three-fourths full of must for red wine, and that the must is " normal " as regards sugar-content and acidity.

The top of the vat is covered with a clean cloth (a bridge-table cover is just the right size, and it looks a lot more attractive atop a fermenting-vat than it does on a bridge-table), and the must is left to its own devices. The temperature of the must should be as close to 80° F. as possible, in order to assure a rapid development of the yeast.[1]

At the end of twelve hours the cloth should be removed and the must thoroughly stirred. It may show signs of activity; it may not. The cloth should then be replaced.

The must is stirred morning and evening thereafter.

[1] It is assumed that the wine-maker is not going to bother with a starter of actively fermenting selected yeast. Those who want to try it, however, may rely upon the following method. Pasteurize two quarts of grape must by heating in a double-boiler to 140° F. and maintain heat for ten minutes. Cool sterile must to room temperature or slightly above, pour into one-gallon bottle, and add yeast culture. Plug with cotton and put in a warm place. After twenty-four hours add another quart of sterile must. At the end of the second day the starter will be in violent fermentation and ready to add to the vat. As soon as the grapes are crushed and in the vat, add 30 grammes potassium metabisulphite ($K_2S_2O_5$) for every 16 lugs of crushed grapes, mix thoroughly, and allow to stand for two to four hours. The sulphite should be fresh, as it deteriorates rapidly. The effect of the sulphite is to kill all unwanted organisms. Then add the actively fermenting starter to the sulphited grapes and proceed as above.

At the end of twenty-four hours the characteristic symptoms of fermentation should be apparent. If they are not apparent at the end of forty-eight hours, measures should be taken to stimulate the fermentation.

The simplest method of stimulating fermentation is to fill a clean bucket half full of fairly hot water and lower it gently into the must. It will be supported by the superior density of the must, but it should be secured, by means of a piece of light rope, to a strong stick or board that is placed across the top of the vat. The warm water should be renewed occasionally.

Another method is to remove a pailful of the must and place the pail in a tub of fairly hot water until the must is well warmed through, and then to return the must to the vat.

These drastic measures are seldom necessary unless the temperature of the must is very low. They always bring results.

When fermentation is well under way, the chapeau will be found to have risen considerably, so that most of the empty one-fourth of the barrel is filled. That is why the barrel was only filled three-fourths full in the first place. Better to err on the side of conservatism, for an overflow can cause a dreadful mess.

The chapeau should not be allowed to touch the cloth; if it does, the cloth should be renewed immediately, for a damp cloth is paradise for the germs of acetic fermentation. A cautious thing to do is to drill a number of holes in the barrel-head which was removed at the making of the vat, and when the fermentation is going well, to place this over the open top of the vat as a loose cover, throwing the cloth over this. It is naturally just the right size for the purpose. This not only keeps the cloth from sagging, but helps, in cold weather, to retain the heat of fermentation, and also allows a cap of carbon dioxide to form over the

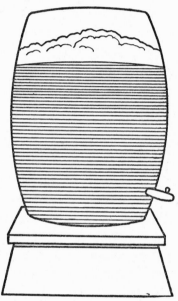

Open Fermentation

top of the fermenting mass. This cap of gas prevents the free access of air to the must, once the fermentation is well started, and so helps to keep out the acetic germs.

The cover should be removed and the chapeau broken up every morning and evening during the period of violent fermentation.

Instead of this open method of vinification, a combination of open and submerged (see Chapter IV) may be adapted to small-scale wine-making. The perforated barrel-top is trimmed down about half an inch all around so that it slips easily in and out of the barrel.

Submerged Fermentation

When fermentation is well under way, this is placed on the chapeau, and the chapeau thus pushed beneath the surface. The barrel-top is held in place by cleats previously affixed to the inside of the vat, under which it is slipped, or by means of oak wedges, as illustrated.

The temperature of the must rises considerably during fermentation. It is advisable not to let it get above

[168

85° F. If the temperature of the room is subject to control, this is fairly easy. Otherwise one may only agonize.

It is advisable to take a reading with the saccharometer each evening, when the chapeau is broken up. This will give an accurate notion of the advancement of the fermentation. Many wine-makers keep a record of these readings, which are used as a basis for meditation during the winter months. A small notebook for the pertinent facts, such as date of vintage, sugar-content and acidity of must, speed of fermentation, etc., may be kept with profit.

THE PRESSING

When the saccharometer indicates that all but four per cent of the sugar has been converted into alcohol and carbon dioxide, the time has come to separate the new wine from the marc. The elapsed time between the crushing of the grapes and the pressing of the new wine varies from three days to two weeks; it seldom takes more than five days.

Preparing the Equipment. The *press* should be scrubbed with a strong hot solution of washing soda and well rinsed in warm and cold water. The *five-gallon glass bottles* should be washed with the same solution and thoroughly rinsed. So should the *two enamelled pails* and the *funnel*. The *two pressing bags* should be sterilized by boiling.

If kegs are to be used instead of five-gallon glass bottles, the process of preparing them is more elaborate. The keg is partly filled through the bung-hole with warm water and left standing for a day or two. This water is then emptied, and the keg is thoroughly rinsed with a hot solution of washing soda. It is then rinsed with fresh water. If the keg has held wine before, it must in addition be sulphured. This is done by placing a sulphur match (which may be bought at any drug store) in a metal holder, lighting the match, lowering the holder through the bung-hole so that it hangs in the keg, and then bunging the keg lightly. The fumes of sulphur dioxide given off by the match sterilize the keg. The holder for the match must be so fashioned as not to allow any of the burnt match to fall into the keg, for it will give a bad taste to the wine.

Drawing Down. This is merely a fancy name for the operation of draining off through the spigot as much wine as will drain. In theory this is very easy to do: one simply places a pail beneath the spigot and turns the spigot's handle. Unfortunately the practice is made more difficult by the fact that the spigot usually gets clogged by a grape skin, and unclogging a spigot can only be compared in difficulty with unscrambling an egg. Not even that handiest of all tools, a bent wire, will unclog it satisfactorily. The accepted method of keeping the spigot clear is to pack clean straw (not excelsior) in a cheese-cloth bag and to tie this around the inside end of the spigot before the vat is filled. This, in theory, keeps the grape skins out and lets the juice through. If the bag is not displaced during the upheaval of fermentation, this sometimes works.

If the wine-maker is lucky and actually succeeds in

drawing down a good bit of his wine, he pours it into the first of his five-gallon bottles, meanwhile allowing the spigot to pour into his second pail. The bottle should be filled to the neck; the mouth is then wiped dry with a clean cloth, and a plug of clean absorbent cotton inserted as a temporary bung.

When all has drained that will drain, the spigot is closed, and the pressing begins. One of the buckets is placed in position to catch the press wine as it flows from the bed of the press. With the other bucket as a bailing instrument, its outside thoroughly rinsed off, a pressing bag is filled with the saturated marc which remains in the fermenting-vat. The bag should not be filled too full, or it will slop over. The bag is quickly transferred to the press, and the top of the bag is folded over. The wooden pressing block is then placed over the bag, and the screw is brought down. Wine will immediately begin to flow from the bed of the press into the pail. Pressure should not be applied too rapidly, but one need not worry about pressing too hard. A wooden club is furnished with every press, by which a greater leverage may be obtained.

When the first pressing is finished, the screw should be brought up again, the bag of pressed (and apparently dry) marc taken out, and the packed mass thoroughly loosened. This is then replaced for a second pressing. Some even give the marc a third pressing, but when small quantities are being made, the yield of a third pressing is hardly enough to warrant the trouble. When all of the juice has been pressed, the dry marc is emptied from the bag into a tub. A " second " wine is made from the marc, as described in Chapter ix. The bag is refilled, and the operation is repeated until all is pressed. The extra bag is insurance against faulty seams. Nothing is more tragic than to have a pressing bag spring a serious leak in the middle of the pressing, and to have no substitute.

The drawn wine, being less harsh than the press wine, is usually kept separate. The press wine, however, is in no sense poor wine. It simply requires more aging before it loses its harshness. The five-gallon bottles should be filled to the neck; if part of a bottle of drawn wine is left over, it should be filled with press wine. Partially filled bottles are very apt to turn to vinegar.

If the fermenting-vat has no spigot, or if the spigot gets plugged up, simply eliminate the drawing down and press the entire mass. It will of course be much more liquid — and the pressing in consequence somewhat more messy — but it is pressed in just the same way. When the drawing down is not done, the quality of the wine is uniform, and there are consequently fewer fractional quantities to deal with.

When the pressing is finally finished, the mouth of each five-gallon bottle should be wiped very carefully with a clean, dry cloth, and a plug of absorbent cotton wadded in. These bottles should not be corked, as the wine is still fermenting and corks will be promptly blown out. The absorbent cotton lets the gas out, but does not let in impurities from the air.

The bottles of newly pressed wine are then set aside until time for the first racking. A two-story wooden rack, two five-gallon bottles deep, saves space if a considerable quantity of wine is being made. Otherwise any bench or sturdy shelf will do. It is best not to keep the bottles on the floor, since the floor is seldom the same temperature as the room, and the temperature of the wine should be uniform.

The new wine is now made. During the process of fermentation, and especially at the time of pressing, the wine-maker will doubtless have tasted it. Unless he is forewarned, he will be disappointed. During the course of fermentation it will be sickly sweetish, with a faintly disgusting aftertaste. At the time of pressing it will still be faintly sweetish and will also be harsh and raw, and in addition will be muddy with yeast and other suspended matter. But that need cause no alarm, for though the must has now definitely been transformed into wine, that wine will not be fit to drink until much more has happened and much time has passed. Patience will have its reward.

Subsequent care of the new red wine is identical with that of new white wine. It is discussed in Chapters vii and viii.

Chapter Six

WHITE WINE

WHITE wine is made of grapes which are pressed before fermentation; it is not fermented on the skins, as red wine is. Since the colouring matter of most varieties of grapes is in the skins and is extracted only during fermentation, white wine may consequently be made from dark grapes if the skins are not left in contact with the juice. The rich dark Burgundies are made from the Pinot grape. Champagnes, which are effervescent white wines, are also made from the Pinot grape. Burgundies are fermented on the skins; Champagnes are not.

Of course, it does not follow that *all* dark grapes yield a good white wine; the white wines made from some of them, although sound, are so definitely inferior to the red wines which they yield that they are never used. And no one ever made any white wine at all from the varieties called *teinturiers*, the dark varieties which have pigment in their juice as well as in their skins. It is well to remember that white wines are more delicate, and consequently require more care in the making, than red.

[174

WHITE WINE

As a general rule, it is harder to buy suitable varieties of California white-wine grapes than it is to buy good red-wine grapes. There is less demand for them, for one thing, and it so happens that the white-wine varieties are mostly thinner-skinned and do not stand shipment so well. The following varieties are those most frequently shipped:

Thompson's Seedless. The correct name for Thompson's Seedless (though not the name under which it is shipped) is Sultanina. It is also known as the Oval Kishmish in the Levant, and the Sultana in South Africa and Australia. It is a grape of many uses, and many thousands of acres are given over to it in California. It is a small oval grape, varying in colour from green to yellow and sometimes even showing a trace of pink, and its bunches are enormous, frequently more than a foot long. It is primarily a seedless raisin grape. It is also shipped in vast quantities for table use. That, as a matter of fact, is why it is always available in the markets. Its sugar-content averages around twenty-four per cent, and its acidity is medium. The wine made from Thompson's Seedless is pale straw in colour and is sound and potable, but without any marked character. I am told that it much resembles some of the light white wines of Hungary. Whether it does or not I do not know.

Muscat. The name of Muscat is here included as a warning, for it is exceedingly plentiful in the markets, and the temptation will be to try it. There are several varieties of Muscat, the Muscat of Alexandria being the most common, but they are shipped under one name, and the maker of dry wines may be quite impartial in consigning them all to the same perdition. The Muscat is primarily a raisin grape; it is very high in sugar, frequently running over thirty per cent, and this makes absolutely impossible the production of dry wine from them without extravagant watering. All varieties of Muscat have a very pronounced musky, or leonine, odour and flavour about which there can be no doubt or confusion. The Italians use them in great quantities for making a heavy sweet wine of maximum alcoholic content, which some later fortify still further with alcohol.

Malaga. This is also included as a warning, for it is very plentiful in the market. For years it was the most popular of the California table grapes, but in 1932 the shipments of Thompson's Seedless finally overtook it. It is much too sweet for the making of dry wine without a great deal of watering. It is not the grape from which the true Malaga wines are made.

Golden Chasselas. This is the name which is given to several very similar varieties, all of which yield excellent white wines which are of a deep golden colour and possess a very agreeable bouquet. It is the best of the varieties that are shipped in considerable quantity, but it may not be compared in quality to some of the varieties that are not shipped. Its sugar-content runs slightly over twenty-two per cent, and its acidity is normal.

Mission. This grape is described in the list of red-

[176

wine grapes. It yields a good white wine if its sugar-content is not too high.

Zinfandel. A white wine may be made from Zinfandel, but it seldom is.

The following excellent varieties are seldom seen in the Eastern markets, and, indeed, their acreage in California has been greatly reduced since prohibition, in contrast to the increase in acreage set to the most popular red-wine varieties.

Burger. Sixteen cars of Burger were shipped east during 1932. It is used for making light white wines in the " hock " style, very delicate and refreshing. It is grown a good deal in Germany, but is there considered inferior to the Riesling. It is very juicy, and its compact bunches tend to get mouldy; that is one reason why it is seldom shipped.

Palomino. This is frequently confused with Golden Chasselas. It is of Spanish origin, and one of the two grapes which predominate in the sherries. Its sugar-content is apt to be too high for the making of a light dry wine; but if not, it gives superb results.

Pedro Ximenes. Also Pedro Jiminez. It is the other Spanish sherry grape. It, too, is apt to be too high in sugar for the production of a thoroughly fermented dry wine. There is some doubt whether the grape grown in California is the true Pedro Ximenes or a first cousin to it.

Riesling. For those partial to Rhine wines, the Riesling is the queen of all vines, not even excepting the classic growths of the Gironde and the Bourgogne.

The several Riesling varieties — of which there are three, Franken Riesling, Johannisberg Riesling, and Chauché Gris or Grey Riesling — are also the finest white-wine grapes grown in California. They are all of German origin, and it is from them, and nothing else, that the very finest of the Rhine wines are made. They are all highly aromatic and yield the characteristic Rhine-wine bouquet. Franken and Johannisberg have a medium sugar-content and are rather high in acid. Chauché Gris normally has a higher sugar-content than the other two, and less acidity. They are practically never found in the Eastern markets, though the freshly pressed and frozen juice is sometimes shipped.

Sauvignon. In France the Sauvignon is extensively planted in the Sauternes district, where it is one of the two grapes which are usually blended in the making of the liquorous Sauternes wines. In making Sauternes it is allowed to hang on the vines until it is over-ripe and has been attacked by the *pourriture noble,* or " noble rot." It is this rot which gives the wine its characteristic flavour. Sauvignon used to be planted quite considerably in California, but most of it has been uprooted in favour of the grosser plants and only gets into the Eastern markets by accident.

Semillon. This is the other, and perhaps the more famous, of the two Sauternes grapes — " le grand cépage blanc français." It is hard to ship successfully.

Traminer. After the Rieslings this is perhaps the best of the German wine grapes. It has many other names, the best-known being Savagnin and Fränkischer. Per-

old says that it is the grape from which Klosterneu-
burger, Diedesheimer, and several other well-known
Rhenish wines are made. There was formerly a considerable acreage of it in California, but the acreage
has declined.

NATIVE WHITE-WINE GRAPES

Good native white-wine varieties are more plentiful in the markets than good native red-wine varieties.
True, they are not nearly so plentiful as the ubiquitous
Concord, but if an eye is kept cocked toward the
markets, it is always possible to find some Catawbas or
Delawares. In the Northern and Eastern states the native varieties ripen around the middle of October and
are not in the market for long. In the Southern states
they ripen somewhat earlier. Since these varieties,
with the exception of the Catawba and the Delaware,
are grown only for local markets, descriptions of them
are all set down in alphabetical order. Some of them
can be found by nosing about the country-side (the
nosing ought to be done during September or earlier,
so that plans may be laid). Those who have the urge
to grow their own grapes should consult the Appendix for information as to the best varieties for each
grape-growing region.

Brighton. This grape, which is a dusty red in colour,
is a hybrid of *labrusca* and a variety of *vinifera*. It is
one of the comparatively few of such hybrids which
has not inherited the worst characteristics of both.
It is grown considerably in New York State for
blending to make sparkling white wines. It is not

179]

much grown elsewhere. Most nurserymen stock this variety.

Catawba. Enough has been said in Chapter ii to indicate that Catawba is a very serviceable plant. This is also a reddish grape, with a delightful aroma. It was formerly the most popular of all American grapes, being grown in every viticultural region of the country. Its sugar averages about twenty per cent, sometimes running higher; its acidity fluctuates considerably. Catawba wine has a very definite individuality, and like all persons of strong individuality it has its detractors as well as its passionate admirers.

Delaware. This is generally conceded to be the best of the native white-wine grapes. It is also, fortunately, the third most generally grown of the native grapes (Niagara and Concord being, of course, the other two), though we must thank the popularity which it also enjoys as a table grape for this. The bunch is small and compact, and the grapes are a deep pink and covered with a faintly purplish bloom. Its sugar-content runs quite high for a native grape, not infrequently exceeding twenty-two per cent. Its acid-content is variable and really ought to be watched. It was formerly much used in the blending of sparkling white wines; it was also blended for still dry white wines, but many prefer the unblended Delaware, for it sails proudly under its own sprightly bouquet and delicate flavour.

Diamond (*Moore's*). This is, like Brighton, a successful *labrusca-vinifera* hybrid, and it holds the same place among the green grapes that Brighton holds among the red. It used to be a great favourite in central New York State in blending for the sparkling wines. It is also satisfactory as a still wine, but since it does not ship well, it is not often found in the markets; one must find a grower. Nurserymen nearly always carry it.

Diana. This is a reddish grape which is not unlike Catawba, both in appearance and in the quality of the fruit. The flavour is similar to that of the Catawba, but somewhat less assertive. Its sugar-content, in the same localities, is about the same as that of the Catawba, but its acidity is apt to be somewhat less.

Dutchess. The blood of four species, *labrusca, bourquiniana, aestivalis,* and *vinifera,* is carried in the vines of Dutchess. When fully ripe it is amber-coloured. The grape is said to yield excellent wine, but it is not a hardy variety and in consequence it is very seldom grown commercially. It is normal as to both sugar-content and acidity.

Elvira. In Missouri the Elvira used to be grown quite extensively for wine-making. It is a cross between *riparia* and *labrusca.* Because of its exceedingly thin skin it is never shipped.

Grein Golden. This grape is, or was, rather considerably grown west of the Mississippi, especially in the Missouri vineyards. It is a large green grape, another of the successful *riparia-labrusca* hybrids.

Iona. An excellent grape, much resembling the Delaware in appearance, but of different parentage. Many consider it the equal of the Delaware for white wine. Its sugar-content averages about twenty per cent, and its acidity is medium.

Missouri Riesling. It contains no *vinifera* blood whatever, and its characteristics as wine are not those of the Rhenish wines, but that does not alter the fact that it is one of the best of the native wine grapes. It acquired its name accidentally. Like Grein Golden, it does not do well in the Northern viticultural districts, and its production has always been confined largely to Missouri.

Noah. This hybrid bears the curious distinction of being better known among European wine-growers than it is among those of the United States. It is one of the varieties which were imported into France as direct producers and for grafting. It is not used much in France any more, as varieties more congenial to the French soils have since been developed for both purposes. It is now grown in Missouri.

Rommel. Rommel is one of the hundreds of varieties which were produced by T. V. Munson at Denison, Texas. It is highly recommended, but it does not reach full and satisfactory maturity in the North.

Salem. This grape, which appears fairly frequently in the market, is recommended by Rose for white wine. It is a red grape. Its sugar-content rarely gets above twenty per cent, and its acidity, according to Alwood, is satisfactory for wine-making. Hedrick is very enthusiastic about it generally, but does not mention it as a wine grape.

Scuppernong. The most popular of all the Southern Muscadines. It appears in Northern markets occasionally, in quart strawberry-baskets, at prices ranging from twenty-five to forty cents a basket, and is there bought only by nostalgic Southerners. In Virginia and the Carolinas it is very cheap. The berries are large, green, and speckled with bronze, and since they shell almost as soon as they ripen, they are practically never obtained in clusters. As the Southerners make Scuppernong wine, it is heavy and sweet. Its sugar-content is not naturally high, however, and a very pale, dry white wine may be made from it. Its aroma is highly assertive and characteristic — so much so that it is not satisfactory for steady use. It is recommended as an interesting specialty.

Triumph. A green grape which requires a long season and hence cannot be grown successfully in the North. Wherever it is grown, it is very highly esteemed for its white wine. It even has its admirers among the French, and when the French admire an American grape, it must be good.

PREPARING THE MUST

Equipment. With the exception of the fermenting-vat, the equipment needed for preparing white-wine must is exactly what is needed for crushing and pressing when making red wine; namely: crusher, press, tub, buckets, pressing bags, five-gallon bottles, siphoning tube, saccharometer and jar, acid-testing equipment (not absolutely necessary), and absorbent cotton.

Procedure. Equipment should be scrupulously clean — washed with a hot solution of washing soda and thoroughly rinsed. The pressing bags should be boiled.

Never stem grapes when making white wine. The reasons for stemming grapes when making red wine have already been discussed, the chief of them being the elimination of excess tannin. But since white wine is not fermented in contact with seeds, skin, and stems, it never has too much tannin; usually it doesn't have enough.

Place the crusher over the tub (wooden laundry-tub, baby's bathtub, large dishpan). Pick over the bunches and toss them into the hopper of the crusher. When the hopper is full, turn the crank and run the grapes through into the tub.

When there is a tubful of freshly crushed grapes, partly fill a pressing bag and place the bag in the basket of the press. Fold over the top of the bag, place on it the wooden pressing block, and press. The juice flows out onto the bed of the press and from there into a waiting pail. The pressure should be applied gradually, but steadily, and to the full pressure allowed by the press. It is very important to press thoroughly because the juice is sluggish and syrupy; the cell structure of the berries is not completely broken in the crushing,[1] and the berries yield their juice reluctantly.

When the first pressing is finished, raise the screw, remove the bag, jounce it around until the mass of berries and stems is well loosened, and press again. In making white wine it is worth while to press a third time.

[1] When red wine is made, the cell structure is broken down during the fermentation, and the pressing is relatively more easy.

When the marc has yielded all of its juice, empty the bag, fill it again, and repeat the process. The marc may be saved for the making of " sugar wine," as described in Chapter ix.

As fast as the buckets are filled with the fresh juice, they should be poured into the five-gallon bottles in which the juice is to ferment. The bottles should be filled only four-fifths full.

When the pressing is finished, the mouths of all the fermenting-bottles should be wiped dry with a clean cloth and plugged with bungs of absorbent cotton.

All equipment used during the crushing and pressing should be washed immediately. This job is much harder if the fresh juice is allowed to become sticky or dry.

TESTING THE MUST

The must should be tested for sugar-content as soon as possible, by means of the saccharometer. This is done as described in Chapter v, page 155. That section might profitably be reread at this point.

The sugar-content having been determined, adjustment should be made by the addition of pure white cane or beet sugar if the must is deficient (or by the addition of water if the must is too sweet). The correct quantity of sugar to add may be computed from the Sugar Table on page 159. It is easier to adjust white-wine must than red, for the juice has already been separated and its quantity is accurately known. The addition of sugar or water is not recommended if the sugar-content falls naturally between twenty and twenty-five per cent, since a sound fermentation may be obtained without it.

At this point the test for acidity should be made, if it is to be made at all. This test is not absolutely necessary, and the novice may prefer not to bother with it for his first season. Yet if he is anxious to eliminate all uncertainty and seeks to make the finest wine possible from the available grapes, he will take the additional trouble to make this test and to adjust with tartaric acid if adjustment proves necessary. The procedure is described in Chapter v, on pages 159–64.

Since white wines are almost invariably deficient in tannin, it is a good rule to remedy this fault as a part of the regular procedure of preparing the must. The correct dose is one gramme of pure tannic acid for every five-gallon bottle of must. It should be dissolved in a cupful of warm water, added directly to the must, and thoroughly stirred in. Even Mr. H. Warner Allen, a purist of the pure, who condemns the addition of sugar with unmeasured scorn, grudgingly admits the propriety of adding tannin. He says: [1] " Of all chemical additions which can be made to wine, a moderate dose of tannin is the least objectionable."

Most large-scale wine-makers make a practice of *clearing* their must before the fermentation begins. This preliminary clarification does not make the must bright and transparent; it merely eliminates such unwanted substances as the dust or vineyard soil which was carried into the must on the grapes, stray skins or pieces of skin, and any other substances which may

[1] *The Romance of Wine*, p. 76.

happen to be suspended in the must and don't belong there. Such substances can adversely affect the delicacy and " freshness " of white wine, whereas the superior robustness of red wine protects them. This is done in a number of ways: by *fining*, with white of egg or gelatine; *mechanically*, by means of a machine

The fresh must should be siphoned from the sediment before fermentation begins

built on the principle of the cream separator or by means of a revolving screen of fine mesh which resembles a gravel-washer in its manner of working; or by *settling* — that is, allowing the must to rest for twelve to twenty-four hours and then racking it into clean containers before the fermentation gets under way.

Although clearing is not absolutely necessary, it is nevertheless worth the effort. For the amateur wine-maker the last method mentioned, that of *settling,* is the simplest. When the must is placed in the bottles after pressing, it will begin to throw down a muddy-looking sediment almost immediately, which may be an inch thick by the end of twelve hours. The must should be racked from this sediment before active fermentation begins, because when that happens, the force of the rising gas promptly lifts all of the sediment and places it in suspension again. When settling is practised in commercial wineries, the commencement of fermentation is artificially delayed by exposing the must to sulphur dioxide gas (SO_2) made by burning sulphur in the container, or by adding potassium metabisulphite. The bisulphite, reacting with the acids in the must, releases SO_2, which in small doses has the property of killing the bad ferments and rendering temporarily inactive the *saccharomyces.* This practice is allowed under the French law. For the amateur wine-maker the correct dose of potassium metabisulphite to use in connection with settling is two grammes for every five-gallon bottle of must.

THE FERMENTATION

The containers are filled only four-fifths full of must in order to avoid the possibility of overflow when the violent fermentation begins.[1]

[1] This is a point of never-ending controversy among œnologists. One school favours filling containers to the brim in order to *encourage* overflowing, on the theory that the must is thus enabled to rid itself

The wine-maker should, if possible, see that the temperature of the fermenting-room is not too high. The usual practice is to ferment white wines at temperatures somewhat lower than the temperatures of red wines. However, in order to secure a strong start, it is advisable to keep the temperature at first around 80° F.[1]

After an interval varying from eight hours to several days, the violent fermentation begins. The first symptom is the appearance of clots of fine foam on the surface of the liquid, and a rim of bubbles around the edge, which is followed by the gradual rising and diffusion of the sediment which has settled at the bottom of the container. The clots of foam coalesce very rapidly, and within a few hours there develops a thick layer of tiny bubbles. The French describe this by saying that " *le moût forme sa couronne.*" Sometimes, instead, the bubbles are enormous, like the soap bubbles which children blow, and completely fill the empty space at the top of the bottle. Whether the bubbles are large or small depends upon the viscosity of the must, and that varies, of course, according to the character of the grapes.

---

of impurities which might be harmful to the wine. The opposing school objects, and quite convincingly so far as I am concerned: (1) that this is a thoroughly messy practice, and that its principal effect is to attract flies and encourage souring; (2) that the " impurities " thrown off are mostly valuable yeasts; and (3) that much potential wine is lost.

[1] If the wine-maker plans to use a starter of selected yeast, he should refer to the foot-note on page 165 for directions.

A bubbling sound may also be heard at the mouth of the bottle.

When the violent fermentation is well started, the temperature should be lowered, if possible, to around 65° F. and kept there. The danger of the development of bad ferments, which is more to be feared in the making of white wine than of red, is thus kept at a minimum.

Since white wine has not the advantage of the great initial quantity of yeast which is on the skins, its fermentation ordinarily proceeds at a more deliberate pace than that of red wine. Though on occasion it may ferment very rapidly, more usually from two to three weeks, and sometimes more, are required for the conclusion of the initial fermentation.

If fermentation is very slow to start, the must should be warmed. That is done by placing the five-gallon bottle in a wash-tub of warm water and leaving it there for an hour or so, occasionally renewing the warm water.

During fermentation the sugar-content should be tested every few days in order to ascertain the progress of the fermentation.

At intervals the cotton stoppers should be examined. If they have become damp, they should be changed for fresh ones.

The end of the violent fermentation is indicated by the reprecipitation of the sediment, or *lees*, which is composed of the original sediment not removed during the settling operation and kept in suspension during fermentation, yeast which has died or ceased to be active, and certain substances which are normally formed during the course of fermentation, chiefly cream of tartar. The end of violent fermentation is also indicated by the saccharometer, which shows o per cent of sugar (actually some traces of sugar are present, which must be fermented during the slow secondary fermentation).

When the violent fermentation has been concluded, the new wine is racked from its gross lees into clean containers, which are filled to the neck. If five-gallon glass bottles are used, it is necessary to have one extra. As soon as a fermenting-bottle has been emptied of its new wine and lees, it may be rinsed and used to receive new wine from the next bottle. When all of the new wine has been racked, the mouths of the bottles are wiped clean and stoppers of absorbent cotton inserted. They are then set aside for the secondary fermentation. Their later treatment is identical with that of red wine, and is discussed in the two following chapters.

IF BLACK GRAPES ARE USED

It so happens that most of the native white-wine grapes are light red or green. But certain California varieties of dark grapes (Mission and Pinot) are sometimes used for making white wine. If these are used, a number of special precautions are necessary.

1. The *teinturiers* must not be used. The result is a reddish wine which the French call *taché*. Many of

the Eastern black grapes have some pigment in their juice, and of the California varieties Alicante Bouschet has the characteristic.

2. The crushing and pressing should be done as rapidly as possible, in order not to allow the must to stay in contact with the pigmented skins any longer than necessary.

3. The grapes used should not be dead ripe. In the Champagne district of France the Pinot grapes are customarily picked a trifle before they reach complete maturity.

4. The juice which flows naturally from the crushed grapes and the juice released by the first pressing should be kept separate from that of the second and third pressings; the latter are apt to show a tinge of colour.

5. Mixed fermentation is sometimes practised when dark grapes are used in making white wine. The grapes are crushed and pressed, and the first juice is fermented after the fashion of white wine. The grapes are then not pressed a second or third time, but are placed in a vat and allowed to ferment after the red-wine fashion. This is worth trying, if only to see how different two wines from the same grapes may be.

6. Clearing is necessary when black grapes are used, in order to eliminate all fragments of pigmented skin. Simple settling for from six to twelve hours will do, with or without the dose (two grammes per five-gallon bottle) of potassium metabisulphite.

7. If in spite of these precautions the new wine shows traces of colour, there are still a number of

methods of getting rid of it. One is based on the fact that the pigment, when oxidized, becomes insoluble and is precipitated; another on the property which bone-black has of absorbing the colouring matter. These various practices, however, require expert manipulation and have the disadvantage that they rid the wine of certain bouquet-making substances along with the colour. The amateur wine-maker had best resign himself to the tinge of colour — which, after all, does not mean that the wine is not sound.

VIN ROSÉ

Wine which is *taché* should be distinguished from *vin rosé*. This latter is a wine made from dark grapes which has been partially fermented on the skins, but has been pressed before the skins have yielded all of their colour. There are several famous *vins rosés;* and their qualities are not those of a red wine, nor yet those of a white.

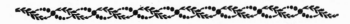

Chapter Seven

THE NEW WINE

It should be apparent by now that vinous fermentation is no simple chemical reaction by which sugar is transformed directly into alcohol and carbon dioxide, but is a very complex series of reactions of which new complexities are constantly being discovered, which has for its end products not merely alcohol and carbon dioxide, but a whole balanced assortment of substances. Careful analyses of newly fermented dry wines have revealed the presence of no less than ten different alcohols (ethyl alcohol, of course, greatly predominating), some twenty-five different acids, both free and in combination, and a large assortment of ethers, aldehydes, and other compounds. The exact proportion in which these occur — and, indeed, the presence or absence of some of them — depends upon the variety and condition of the grapes, the success with which fermentation is carried out, and the strain of yeast which did the actual work. Consequently the chemical composition of two wines is seldom the same. The composition of a typical fresh must was given on page 107. Its composition when newly transformed

[194

into wine is quite different. Maumené [1] gives the following typical analysis of a light, dry, natural wine. The letter F. indicates new compounds formed during fermentation.

	Per cent
Water	89 to 90
Ethyl Alcohol F.	7 to 8

	Per cent
Other Alcohols (Butyl, Amyl, etc.) F.	
Ethers F	
Aldehydes F	
Essential Oils	
Grape Sugar	2 to 3
Mannite F., Mucilages, Gums, Dextrines, Pectin, Fatty Substances	
Oenocyanin	
Glycerine F.	

Saccharomyces ....

Salts — Organic:
- Potassium bitartrate (.55 minimum)
- Tartrate of Calcium and of Ammonia
- Acid Tartrate of Alumina and of Iron
- Racemates
- Acetates, Propionates, Butyrates, Lactates, etc. F.

Salts — Inorganic:

	combined with
Sulphates	Potassium
Nitrates	Sodium
Phosphates	Calcium
Silicates	Magnesium
Chlorides	Aluminium
Bromides	Iron
Iodides	Ammonium
Fluorides	

(Salts 2 to 3)

[1] Quoted by André L. Simon in *The Blood of the Grape*, p. 52.

Per cent

Free acids	Carbonic (.25 maximum) Tartaric and Racemic Malic Citric Tannic Metapectic F. Acetic F. Lactic F. Succinic F. Butyric F. Valeric F.	2 to 3

Such analyses as this are interesting and important to the scientist, but practical wine-makers do not make them for two reasons: first, because they are beyond the abilities of anyone but a trained laboratory technician, and, second, because they are unnecessary. But in commercial wineries certain simpler analyses are customarily made, and although the amateur wine-maker need not bother with these, he is nevertheless better off if he knows them and if he understands their purpose. And if his interest in wine-making becomes something more than utilitarian, he may find it amusing and instructive to try them out.

The usual analyses are four in number: for *alcoholic content*, for *acidity*, for *dry extract*, and for *tannin*.

DETERMINING ALCOHOLIC CONTENT

Alcohol is, literally as well as figuratively, the vital element of the wine. It is that which gives to wine its stimulating quality, and it is an important element in the wine's bouquet and flavour. After water, it is present in larger quantity than any other substance or group of substances. Without at least nine per cent of alcohol, wine is apt to be flat and disagreeable to the taste.[1] Furthermore, with less than nine per cent of alcohol, it is sickly and unstable, cannot be transported safely, will not keep, and cannot even be bottled with any assurance and without the help of artificial preservatives. The importance of having a sufficient quantity of alcohol is obvious.

In determining the degree of alcohol in his wine, the amateur wine-maker has one rule of thumb which suffices him ordinarily. It is this:

Every two per cent of sugar in the must yields approximately one per cent of alcohol in the wine. So if the quantity of sugar in the original must has been determined (with the saccharometer), the degree of alcohol in the finished wine has been roughly determined in advance.

Yet there are occasions when it may be desirable to determine the alcoholic content of the finished wine with greater exactitude. Then the wine must be analysed. The method of analysis here given is that recommended for determining the alcoholic content of wine by the Association of Official Agricultural Chemists (with a few slight modifications).

Equipment. One 300 c.c. *Pyrex flask* and *glass condenser* or "*worm*" (as illustrated); one 100 c.c.

---

[1] This will be corroborated by anyone who has tried any of the 3.2 per cent "wines."

graduated beaker; one *hydrometer for light liquids;* one *hydrometer jar.*[1]

Procedure. Measure 100 c.c. of the wine in the beaker and place it in the flask. Measure 50 c.c. of water and add that to the wine in the flask. If the wine is acetous, add a small quantity of sodium hydroxide (NaOH) to neutralize the acid. Attach the condenser to the flask and fill the cooling space of the condenser

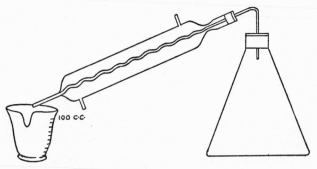

Flask and Condenser for Determining Alcoholic Content

with cold water. Rinse the beaker and place it at the lower end of the condenser. Heat the flask over a gas or alcohol burner. Vapour will commence to pass into the coil, where it will be condensed and drop gradually into the beaker. The condensing bath should be replaced occasionally with more cold water. Collect *almost* 100 c.c. of the condensate, and to that add

[1] This equipment costs about four dollars; any good druggist will tell you where to get it, or it may be bought from a dealer in laboratory equipment.

enough water to bring it to exactly 100 c.c. This is exactly the volume of the wine originally placed in the flask; but it consists only of the alcohol of the wine plus water with all other substances eliminated. Cool the condensate to about 60° F. and pour it into the hydrometer jar. Insert the hydrometer and take the reading. The percentage of alcohol by weight is determined from this reading by reference to the Specific-Gravity Table on page 201.

Example: Suppose the specific-gravity reading is 0.98319. According to the table, a specific gravity of 0.98319 indicates an alcoholic content of 10.50 per cent by weight or 13 per cent by volume.

DETERMINING ACIDITY

The acidity of wine is of two kinds, that which is furnished by the *fixed acids* which were present in the must previous to fermentation and are still in the wine unchanged after fermentation; and that of the *volatile acids*, which are products of fermentation.

Tartaric acid, in the form of free acid and also as cream of tartar (potassium bitartrate), is the predominating fixed acid. The cream of tartar is only sparingly soluble in water and is practically insoluble in alcohol. Therefore all during fermentation, as the quantity of alcohol in the must continues to increase, cream of tartar is thrown down as a precipitate. Because of this precipitation, the acidity of the wine is always less than the acidity of the must; its acidity is usually about seventy-five per cent that of the must. As the wine ages or is subjected to low temperatures, it throws down still more of its cream of tartar, thus still further reducing its acidity. The "mellowness" of old wines is largely a consequence of this loss of cream of tartar.

The other fixed acids that are found in appreciable quantities are malic acid and succinic acid. They need not concern us.

The principal volatile acids to be found in new wine are carbonic acid (which gradually escapes as carbon dioxide gas), acetic acid, butyric acid, and propionic acid. A small quantity of these volatile acids is found in all wine, and in small quantities they serve an important role in the development of the *bouquet*. The bouquet, which is not present in a new wine and develops only with aging, is provided by *ethers*, which are the salts formed by the action of the volatile acids on the higher alcohols contained in the wine. Consequently, if there are no volatile acids at all, there will be no true *bouquet*.

But the presence of volatile acids in more than a very small quantity (o.6 gr. per litre, expressed in sulphuric acid,[1] is generally taken as the safe maximum) is invariably a sign of disease. More of this when we come to the discussion of sick wines. Volatile acidity is, as Bernard says, " the pulse which tells at any moment the state of health of the wine."

Determining total acidity. For practical purposes,

[1] Volatile acidity is more often expressed in terms of acetic acid than sulphuric. To convert sulphuric into acetic multiply by 1.22. Example: .6 gr. per litre (sulphuric) x 1.22 = .732 gr. per litre (acetic).

Specific-Gravity Table

(The correspondence between specific gravity and alcoholic content of mixtures of alcohol and water at 60° F.)

Sp. Gr. at 60° F.	Per Cent by vol.	Per Cent by wt.	Sp. Gr. at 60° F.	Per Cent by vol.	Per Cent by wt.
1.00000	0.0	0.00	0.98374	12.5	10.09
0.99925	0.5	0.40	0.98319	13.0	10.50
0.99850	1.0	0.80	0.98264	13.5	10.91
0.99776	1.5	1.19	0.98210	14.0	11.32
0.99703	2.0	1.59	0.98157	14.5	11.73
0.99630	2.5	1.99	0.98104	15.0	12.14
0.99559	3.0	2.39	0.98051	15.5	12.55
0.99488	3.5	2.79	0.97998	16.0	12.96
0.99419	4.0	3.19	0.97946	16.5	13.37
0.99350	4.5	3.60	0.97895	17.0	13.79
0.99282	5.0	4.00	0.97844	17.5	14.20
0.99215	5.5	4.40	0.97794	18.0	14.61
0.99150	6.0	4.80	0.97744	18.5	15.03
0.99085	6.5	5.21	0.97694	19.0	15.44
0.99022	7.0	5.61	0.97645	19.5	15.85
0.98960	7.5	6.02	0.97596	20.0	16.27
0.98899	8.0	6.42	0.97546	20.5	16.68
0.98838	8.5	6.83	0.97496	21.0	17.10
0.98779	9.0	7.23	0.97446	21.5	17.52
0.98720	9.5	7.64	0.97395	22.0	17.93
0.98661	10.0	8.05	0.97344	22.5	18.35
0.98602	10.5	8.45	0.97293	23.0	18.77
0.98544	11.0	8.86	0.97241	23.5	19.19
0.98487	11.5	9.27	0.97189	24.0	19.60
0.98430	12.0	9.68	0.97137	24.5	20.02
			0.97084	25.0	20.44

provided the fermentation is normal, the wine-maker may simply assume that his new wine has 75 per cent of the acidity of the must from which it was made. Thus if his must had an acidity of 9 gr. expressed in sulphuric acid, he may assume that his new wine has an acidity of between 6 and 7 gr. sulphuric. If he wants to make sure, however, he may determine the acidity of the wine by the same test used in determining the acidity of the must (see page 159), *except* that the new wine should first be heated slightly and shaken in order to drive off all carbon dioxide.

Determining volatile acidity. Since the volatile acidity is the " pulse " of the wine, revealing its state of health, it is sometimes desirable to know just what it is. Unfortunately that is very hard to determine without complicated and expensive apparatus and a considerable degree of laboratory experience. But if there is reason to believe that disease is developing in the wine, the wine-maker may find out indirectly whether the volatile acidity is increasing. For if the wine is healthy, its total acidity tends to decrease rather than increase (thanks to the precipitation of cream of tartar). So if the *total acidity* of the wine, determined as above, turns out to be *greater* than 75 per cent of the acidity of the must, then he may infer that the volatile acidity is higher than it should be. Luckily the amateur has another and still simpler means of discovering whether his wine is diseased, and that is the testimony of his nose. For the various volatile acids have highly pungent and characteristic odours. Acetic acid, which is the one most to be feared, is vinegar, nothing less.

Propionic acid has an odour which much resembles that of acetic acid. Butyric acid smells like rancid butter (it is, indeed, the same substance that gives rancid butter its disagreeable odour). Thus, if the volatile acids increase much beyond the danger point, they have a way of announcing themselves unmistakably.

The following means of determining volatile acidity, devised by W. V. Cruess and R. W. Bettoli, calls for less apparatus than most. By means of it the volatile acidity is determined indirectly: that is, the total acidity and the fixed acidity are determined, and the volatile acidity is determined by subtracting one from the other.

First decolorize 75 c.c. of the wine by allowing it to stand with bone-black which is free from carbonates. Bone-black absorbs the colouring matter. Impure bone-black containing carbonates cannot be used. The decolorized wine is filtered and should be water-white. Titrate 20 c.c. of this wine with .1 normal sodium hydroxide (NaOH). Record the c.c. of NaOH used for titrating and call this "A." Then take 20 c.c. more of the decolorized sample and mix with approximately 2 grammes of common salt (NaCl) in a 200 c.c. Erlenmeyer flask. Boil down this liquid rapidly on a gas or alcohol flame until a copious separation of NaCl takes place and the wine begins to patter. Then pour into the flask 20 c.c. of distilled water and boil down until the NaCl separates again. Dilute this remaining liquid again with distilled water to a volume of 20 c.c. and titrate with .1 normal NaOH. Record the c.c. used for titration and call this "B." Then:

(A — B) x .3 = volatile acid grammes per litre expressed as acetic.

The factor .3 is explained as follows: 1 c.c. of .1 normal NaOH = .006 gramme acetic acid. If a 60 c.c. sample were used, the factor would be .1 because

$$\frac{\text{c.c. NaOH x .006}}{60} \text{ x 1000 becomes c.c. NaOH x .1 in}$$

calculating the grammes of acetic acid per 1,000 c.c. (litre) of wine. Since our sample is one-third of 60, or 20 c.c., the factor is three times as large, or .3.

Equipment needed: burner, Erlenmeyer flasks, 20 c.c. pipettes, 3-inch glass funnel, filter paper, burette graduated in .1 c.c., supply of .1 NaOH, pure bone-black, indicator (either litmus or phenolphthalein solution).

DRY RESIDUE

The dry residue, or extract, is that which is left after a measured quantity of the wine has been carefully and completely evaporated. This residue contains an assortment of acids, gummy substances, unfermented sugar, inorganic salts, etc., and in natural dry wines it varies from 17 to 30 grammes per litre. Red wines, with their tannin and colouring matter, naturally yield a larger quantity of dry residue than do white wines. The amateur wine-maker never has any need for determining the amount of dry residue which his wine will yield, for the reason that the information is of no particular interest or value to him. Interest in it is confined to experimental chemists, to wine-merchants, and to guardians of the public health. The chemists are interested because analysis of the residue tells them things about the processes of fermentation. The merchants and guardians are interested because by determining the exact proportion of dry residue they may often detect certain frauds, such as the practice of making a given quantity of wine go farther by adding alcohol and water to it. Such a practice naturally reduces the proportion of dry extract. It is perhaps characteristic of an acquisitive society that there should be available commercially a " dry residue " to be added to such false wines.[1]

TANNIN

Something has already been said of the importance of tannin as a constituent of wine. It is important because it definitely inhibits the development of certain diseases, because it helps the wine to clarify naturally by combining with and precipitating the albuminous matter which new wines always contain in suspension, and because of the little-understood but definitely important part which it plays in the phenomena of aging. The quantity of tannin varies tremendously not only from one wine to another, but even during the life of any given bottle. It is always sufficient in red wines, which get it from skin, seeds, and stems during fermentation, and nearly always deficient in white wines. If white-wine must receives its dose of tannin before fermentation, however (see page 186), the normal deficiency in this respect need cause no concern. The test for tannin is rather difficult and involves the careful preparation of a number of re-

[1] The official methods of determining dry extract are to be found in the *Methods of Analysis*, edited by a Committee of the Association of Official Agricultural Chemists; Third edition, Washington, 1930; p. 138.

agents; the amateur wine-maker will have no occasion to use it.[1]

IMPROVING THE NEW WINE

The preceding sections of this chapter have been devoted to a brief summary of the principal constituents of a new wine and of the qualities which they contribute to what might be called the " harmony " of the whole. In general it is a good rule not to try to adjust deficiencies in the wine — discords in the harmony, if you prefer — by artificial means. The only method of improving a wine that is clearly and completely above reproach is that of blending. All others are to be viewed with suspicion.

Alcohol. If the new wine is definitely deficient in alcohol, the only legitimate and satisfactory method of making a potable drink out of it and assuring its stability and a decently long life is that of *blending with a wine of higher alcoholic content.* The practice of raising its alcoholic content by adding alcohol to it cannot be too strongly discouraged. The French law, which is very enlightened on the subject of wines and wine-making, expressly forbids this (*vinage*) except for wines made for the export trade [2] and for the fortification of liqueur wines. But if the wine-maker has adjusted the sugar-content of his must in the first place, he can be pretty sure that his wine will have a satisfactory alcoholic content.

Acidity. If the new wine has an excessively high

---

[1] The official test is to be found in *Methods of Analysis*, p. 141.
[2] The Gallic touch.

degree of acidity — as may occasionally happen if the grapes used are not thoroughly ripe — the obvious thing to do is to blend it with a wine low in acidity. It is possible to reduce the acidity by dosing with *neutral potassium tartrate*, but the practice is not recommended. If one has no low-acid wine suitable for blending, the thing to do is to wait; time will eliminate the harshness or greenness.

If the wine is low in acidity, the best thing to do is to blend it with a wine having plenty of acidity (but never with wine that is acetic!). In the absence of such a blending wine, it is permissible to raise the acidity by the addition of either pure *tartaric acid* or pure *citric acid*.

Suppose the acidity of the new wine is 2 grammes per litre (sulphuric). The wine-maker wants to add enough tartaric acid to raise the acidity to 5 gr. per litre (sulphuric) — in other words to add a quantity of tartaric acid equivalent to 3 gr. per litre expressed in sulphuric. Sulphuric acid is 1.53 times as " acid " as tartaric. Therefore 3 gr. (sulphuric) x 1.53 = 4.59 gr. (tartaric). A dose of 4.59 gr. pure tartaric acid per litre will therefore give the desired acidity.[1] The tartaric acid should be pure and should be dissolved in a little of the wine before it is added, then thoroughly mixed.

In France the use of tartaric acid is forbidden for this purpose, not because it is unsatisfactory, but because it is all too satisfactory. The fabricators of fake wines make great use of it. Consequently the French

[1] 1 gallon = 3.78 litres.

law authorizes the use of pure citric acid instead. The procedure is precisely the same, except that sulphuric acid is only 1.4 times as " acid " as citric.

But it is better to blend a flat wine with an acid wine, if that is possible, and if the acidity of the must has been properly adjusted in the first place, there is no danger of a shortage of acidity in the wine.

Blending. The practice of blending is, then, far and away the best and safest means of improving or ameliorating a wine which has constitutional defects. It is a practice which is quite unexceptionable and is honoured by long tradition. There are very few wines — and those only of the choicest growths — which cannot be improved by means of it, provided, of course, that the blending is intelligently done.

On its lowest scale blending can be almost a mechanical procedure. Given a wine of such-and-such alcoholic content, how much of it must be blended with another wine of such-and-such content to secure a blend of normal vinosity? A few moments of elementary arithmetic will yield the answer.

Likewise given a flattish wine of such-and-such a degree of acidity and another harsh wine of such-and-such acidity, in what proportions must they be combined to yield a wine of " normal acidity " — that is, a wine that is fresh and " clean," but not harsh to the palate? Anyone may figure that out.

Or, again, let us assume that we have a red wine that rather lacks colour. The obvious procedure is to blend it with a wine which has a very deep colour.

The advantages of blending two wines of complementary qualities are now so widely recognized that many wines are made on a vast scale with the deliberate intention of using them for blends. Thus, in the Midi and in Algeria the French have enormous vineyards for the production of cheap grapes; the wines from these are sent to Bordeaux or other great shipping points and blended with the finer growths. Thus are produced vast quantities of wine of a fair quality having some of the qualities of the finer wines. Every important shipper has his "monopole" or house brand, which is a wine blended so as to possess certain definite characteristics year in and year out.

Only experience can give skill in the blending of wines. But the following points will help one to gain experience without encountering disaster:

1. When undertaking to blend, it is a good idea first to blend a small quantity in a graduated glass beaker, noting the quantity of each wine which goes into the blend, and to put this in a small bottle, corked, for twenty-four hours, then to try by smelling and tasting. Allowance must be given for the fact that no wine at the blending stage after the first racking (that is, in December) is really fit to drink. If, allowing for this, the sample blend is otherwise satisfactory, the major operation may be performed.

2. The wines entering into a blend should all be absolutely sound — that is, wines which have undergone a healthy fermentation and show no signs of disease. The outcome of a blend of a sound wine with an unsound one can only be disastrous.

3. In the United States, wines from the native grapes, which as a rule are rather low in sugar and high in acidity, will blend well with wines from California grapes, which are somewhat higher in sugar and lower in acidity.

4. The wines to be blended should be of approximately the same age.

5. Never blend a sweet wine with a dry wine.

Yet beyond offering a few simple rules, one may no more convey the art of blending than one may teach the art of writing poetry. Time and again, men have approached wine-making in the matter-of-fact attitude of the chemist, disposed to " debunk " it, only to recognize in the end that chemistry does not embrace the whole art of skilful wine-making. W. D. Bigelow, at one time Dr. Harvey W. Wiley's chief chemist, put the matter very well. " What we need in this laboratory," he said, speaking of the Food and Drug Administration's work in wines, " is a wine-maker with a cultivated taste and smell. Chemistry carries us just so far and no farther, when we are dropped off as from a precipice. We require a cultivated sense of smell and taste to determine the excess or lack of different properties in a wine, and what different varieties of grapes or wines will blend or marry, so as to develop into a fine wine." He could hardly have chosen an analogy more apt than that of marriage — an institution which is full of disconcerting traps for scientists and rationalists — for a successful blend is a delicate balance of imponderables. It is like a marriage in which the weaknesses of a wife who is *racée, très recommandée,* but *faible* are counterbalanced by a husband who, if tending toward harshness, has at least the virtue of greater strength and stability. A good blend is a happy marriage of wines.

Chapter Eight

THE CARE OF WINES

WHEN the wine, whether red or white, has finished its first violent fermentation, a good deal more has still to happen to it before it is worthy to be called a beverage. It has not even finished its fermentation, for, though most of the *saccharomyces* have done their work and sunk to the lees, and though the new wine has lost its sweetness to the taste, traces of grape sugar are still there. It is the task of other *saccharomyces*, working slowly and thoroughly, to clean up after their more impatient predecessors and to convert these remaining traces of sugar into alcohol. Until all of the sugar has been converted, the wine is nervous and unsettled, apt to start in its slumber and to do all sorts of unexpected things.

The care of new wines consists: (1) in providing a suitable environment for this gradual, or secondary, fermentation; (2) in helping the wine to clear itself of all impurities; (3) in preserving the wine from contamination and infection; and (4) in assisting the wine in the processes of aging, by which it loses its youth-

ful roughness and emerges into a well-behaved, generous, and smoothly-rounded maturity.

SECONDARY FERMENTATION

The new wine, if red, has been pressed at the end
of its violent fermentation and placed in five-gallon
glass bottles or proper white oak casks. A water-valve
is then affixed to every container.

The new wine, if white, has been racked from the
bottles or kegs in which it underwent its violent fermentation, into clean containers. The gross lees which
precipitated toward the end of that fermentation have
thus been eliminated. A water-valve is then affixed to
every container.

Water-valves. The purpose of a water-valve is to
allow carbon dioxide to escape from a package of
wine whilst not allowing any air to enter. A tradi-
tionalist is occasionally to be found who heaps ridicule
on those who use this simple and efficient device, for
the reason that water-valves have not always been
known; he advocates, in its stead, the use of some
more romantic device, such as a vine-leaf, an inverted
bung, or a sandbag (what there is romantic about an
inverted bung or a sandbag I do not pretend to know).
It will be found, usually, that these bacchic enthusiasts
have not made wine themselves.

There are many kinds of water-valves, and they
may be bought, or made, at a cost of from five to
seventy-five cents apiece. The glass curlicue type is
fitted into a rubber stopper having a hole of the cor-

rect diameter, or into an ordinary cork which has had a hole burnt through it or drilled through it with an ordinary brace and bit. The stopper and valve should be boiled before being inserted into the bottle-

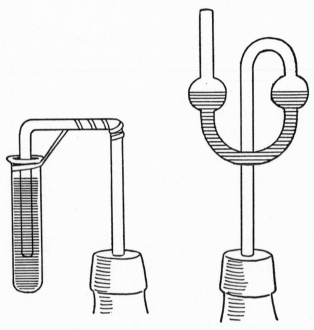

Two Types of Water-valve

mouth or bung-hole. A still simpler valve, also shown in the illustration, may be made at home for about three cents. Buy some ⅜-inch plain glass tubing, which comes in five-foot lengths for a few cents a foot, and some ¾-inch by 6-inch plain glass test-tubes. Break the rod into 1-foot lengths by notching with a file, bend it into a U over the gas stove burner, taking care to heat it gradually and rotate it during the heating. Fit one end of the U with a rubber stopper or cork and attach the test-tube to the other end, as shown, by means of adhesive tape.

When the containers have been fitted with the valves — and it is a good idea to seal the cork with paraffin or sealing-wax — the curlicue type of valve should be half-filled with water, the test-tube type filled so that the end of the U tube is an inch or so under water. The containers are then placed in a suitable cellar, preferably on benches or strong shelves. "Cellar" need not be taken too literally, yet plainly an attic, which is subject to extreme fluctuations of temperature, or a room with a much-used outside door, or a kitchen where high temperatures prevail part of the time and a bitter chill descends during the night are none of them satisfactory. The temperature of new wine should be kept as constant as possible, and the ideal temperature during the course of the secondary fermentation is 65° F.

The course of the secondary fermentation is signified by the regular ascent of bubbles of gas through the water in the valve. The bubbles come thick and fast at first and are accompanied by a gentle gurgling, a sound which falls gratefully upon the ear and has a definitely hypnotic quality. Listening to it may easily become an incurable habit. Wine-makers habitually use it as a sedative for frayed nerves; it is easy under its influence to fall into a brown study — or, as others put it, to become rapt in contemplation

— and not to emerge or become unrapt until hours later.

As the fermentation wears on, these gurgles become less and less frequent and finally cease entirely. Ordinarily the bubbling is just about over by the end of four weeks. An occasional bubble will rise, and sometimes with the coming of warm weather in the spring there is quite a spell of bubbling. But, at any rate, by the end of the first month it is time to *rack*.

RACKING

Racking is the gentle art of separating the wine from its lees. The lees consist of yeasts both good and bad, cream of tartar, albuminous matter, and various other substances which the wine must rid itself of before it becomes bright and clear and drinkable. Racking is then a partial purification. Since it is done repeatedly during the life of the wine, each racking is a further act of purification. Repeated often enough, racking is almost as effective as sterilization. Another reason for racking is that though a wine may become perfectly clear while resting on its lees, a renewed fermentation brought on by warm weather may well lift the lees into suspension again, causing the wine to become turbid and subjecting it to needless dangers from disease ferments. These alarums are naturally not possible if the wine has been separated from its lees.

When to Rack. The first racking should be undertaken about a month after the new wine has been put in its containers for the secondary fermentation. It takes place, therefore, ordinarily about the end of November or early in December.

The wine is racked a second time at the end of February, before the coming of the warm weather, when a renewal of activity in the wine is apt to unsettle it.

The wine is ordinarily racked a third time in June, in order to separate it from the lees which have been formed during the activity of the spring.

The wine is racked a fourth time in October, in order to rid it of any lees which have been thrown down during the hot weather.

Subsequently it is racked twice a year, in the spring and in the fall, until it is bottled.

The day (evening, usually) which is selected for racking should be clear, and a brisk breeze should be blowing. This is not, as was long supposed, a superstition only. When atmospheric pressure is light, the gas which is in solution in the wine tends to be released and to rise to the surface, bringing with it a certain quantity of precipitated matter. Of course the racking ought to be done when the greatest possible quantity of precipitated matter can be left behind.

The First Racking. Racking is not an onerous task; on the contrary, as befits a rite of purification, it is a joyous occasion, to be followed if possible by drinking and feasting. But the prospect of the feast should never be allowed to interfere with the proper performance of the rite. The siphoning hose must be sterilized by boiling, and the container which is to receive the racked wine must be thoroughly cleaned.

The container which is to receive the racked wine naturally has to be placed lower than that from which the wine is being racked; hence the desirability of benches or shelves. If the wine is lifted before the racking, it should be lifted very gently in order to avoid disturbing the lees, and should be allowed to settle again.

Aerate the wine at the first racking

When the containers are in place, a water-valve is removed from one of them. This is done by chipping off all paraffin or sealing-wax, gently pulling out the glass tube, and then removing the cork by inserting a corkscrew into the hole. The cork and the mouth of the container should be wiped very carefully before the cork is pulled. One end of the siphon is then inserted into the wine — not too far down, for that will disturb the lees. The flow is started by the traditional method of sucking, and the wine is directed into the clean container. The wine as it is racked should be allowed to flow from the tube down along the inside of the clean container; this aerates the new wine thoroughly, and aeration is good for it at this first racking. The oxygen in the air gives new vigour to the remaining yeasts for their bout with the last lurking traces of unfermented sugar. Some of the impurities in the wine are oxidized and made insoluble. The aging of the wine is hastened somewhat.

When one of the containers has been emptied, it should be rinsed thoroughly. It is then ready to receive the racked wine from the next container.

At the time of the first racking the wine will have cleared perceptibly, but not completely. Its flavour will be harsh and disagreeable, but it will begin to resemble wine. Its odour will be rather more disagreeable than agreeable, but with a vinous suggestion nevertheless. The novice, on tasting the product of his art, is usually convinced at this point that his wine is dreadful stuff. He is begged to wait and give it a chance.

During the course of the secondary fermentation, wine in kegs will be found to have evaporated considerably. Wine in glass containers will naturally not have evaporated. That is one of the advantages of glass containers. Whatever the type of container, there will of course be a loss in volume corresponding to the amount of the lees.

Treatment After First Racking. When the first

racking has been concluded and the wine is once more in clean, fresh containers (filled full), the water-valves are again inserted. If the containers are glass bottles, they may be replaced on their benches or shelves, not to be touched until the February racking, except for an occasional examination to make sure that the water in the valves has not evaporated. If the wine is being aged in wood, however, it is necessary to remove the water-valves and replace with more wine that which has evaporated. This has to be done once a week during December and January and once every two weeks during February. After the February racking it should be done once a month. *Refilling is absolutely imperative if the wine is in wood.* If this is not done, an air space at the top of the keg provides an ideal place for the development of any disease germs which may still be in the wine. Sometimes the wine withstands such neglect, but more often it turns sour.

Later Rackings. Procedure for later rackings is identical with that of the first, with one exception. The wine should not be aerated, but should be kept out of contact with the air as much as possible. Contact with the air may be minimized very easily by plunging the mouth of the siphon below the surface of the liquid in the container which is being filled. Thus only the surface is exposed. As wines grow older, some of them, especially those which are deficient in tannin (white wine), are affected adversely by oxidation and become discoloured. That is the reason for this precaution.

In the course of the first racking it is hardly possible to avoid bringing over a small quantity of the lees with the wine, especially if kegs are used. But little or no lees will come over with subsequent rackings, for the reason that these later lees are almost entirely

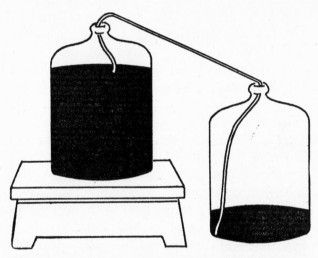

Keep lower end of siphon submerged during later rackings

cream of tartar, which forms crystals and adheres to the bottom of the container. Each racking, also, will show a smaller quantity of lees.

Occasionally it is necessary to rack for special purposes. It is sometimes resorted to in the middle of the secondary fermentation as well as at the end of it, if there is doubt as to the healthy condition of the new wine. Such a racking helps to eliminate as quickly as possible any ferments of disease which may have fallen to the bottom. Racking is also done after *fining* and after *blending*.

FINING

Fining is the art of helping the wine, by the addition of various substances (called *finings*), to clear itself of all suspended matter by precipitation and thus to become perfectly clear and brilliant. A healthy wine will usually clear itself, sometimes very rapidly and even before the secondary fermentation is entirely finished, and sometimes after a more or less prolonged period of gradual precipitation. But often a wine which is otherwise quite healthy and of good report fails to clear itself completely. The French, with their customary precision in all matters pertaining to wine, make nice distinctions between the degrees of turbidity. From the faintly cloudy to the badly muddied they are *vins bleus, vins laiteux, vins louches*, and *vins troublés*. The fact that a wine does not clear itself rapidly does not necessarily signify that it is not healthy. However, so long as material is still in suspension, the health of the wine is in some danger, and it is not particularly pleasing to look upon.

The fining of wine is perfectly legitimate, since it adds nothing to the composition of the wine, and it is sanctioned by immemorial usage. Its effect is not only to clarify the wine and thus to render it more pleasing to the eye, the nose, and the palate, but, by eliminating the suspended matter, to continue the process of purification which is begun by racking. It also has the less desirable effect of removing a little of the colouring matter of red wine and of removing some of the tannin. The latter difficulty is avoided by adding a quantity of tannin at the time of fining equal to the quantity that is going to be removed.

Red wines, being high in tannin, ordinarily clear themselves without any assistance; fining red wines is not recommended unless, by the end of a year, they are yet not candle-bright. The test is simply to hold a candle, in a dark room, behind a glass of the wine; the outline of the flame should be clear and sharp.

White wines are less apt to clear themselves. A simple test of the clarity and brilliance of white wine is that of holding a lighted candle behind a five-gallon bottle of it. If the flame and the fingers which hold the candle show through the bottle in brilliant detail, the wine does not have to be fined. If the outline of candle and fingers is at all fuzzy, the wine should be fined. A good time to fine white wines is immediately after the spring racking.

There are many methods of fining, all of which have their advocates. It is sometimes done by adding kaolin, a silicate which is used in the manufacture of porcelain, or one of several other earths, which combine mechanically with the material in suspension as they settle to the bottom. These are favoured by hasty wine-makers because they settle rapidly. They are often impure, however. Occasionally agar-agar, the popular laxative, is used, by wine-makers who are both hasty and heedless. Neither this nor the earths are recommended.

Fining is more usually done by adding various albuminous substances, which coagulate with the tannin present in the wine and, as they precipitate, drag the suspended matter along with them to the lees. The albuminous substances most commonly used are the serum of fresh beef blood, dried and pulverized blood serum, skimmed milk, and white of egg. Gelatine is also used. Gelatine and white of egg are the favourites, gelatine for white wines, and white of egg for red.

How to Fine Red Wines. Use half the white of one egg for every five gallons of wine to be fined. See that none of the yolk gets into the white. Add to the white of egg a " pinch " of table-salt (one pinch for each half white of egg), and whip in a clean dish until it is moderately stiff. Pour the beaten mixture into the wine to be fined,[1] and stir thoroughly. Another advantage of the five-gallon bottle for small-scale winemaking is here displayed, for the bottle may be picked up, with one clean hand over the mouth, and thoroughly shaken. One shake is equal to five minutes of stirring. In order to facilitate the shake, a quart or so of wine should be removed from the bottle before the white of egg is added, and replaced after the shaking. The mouth of the bottle is then wiped and dried with a clean cloth, and the water-valve replaced. The wine will have become milky, but when it has been replaced on its bench or shelf, the suspended matter will gradually settle. By the end of ten days or two weeks

[1] Beaten white of egg does not really pour; it has to be crowded in.

it should be perfectly clear. It is then racked into a clean container, the water-valve is put in place, and the container put at rest. It is not necessary to add tannin when fining red wine.

How to Fine White Wines. For white wine, gelatine is preferred to white of egg. But since white wines are deficient in tannin, and tannin is always lost in the course of fining, it is the part of caution to make up for the loss in advance. Otherwise the fining is liable not to " take." The procedure is as follows:

Use 3 grammes of the best leaf gelatine and 2.5 grammes of the finest (dry) tannic acid for every five gallons of wine to be fined. Let the druggist weigh it for you. Soak the gelatine in a small quantity of water until it is soft; then, warming it gently on the stove, stir it until it is dissolved. Rack off a quart of wine into each of two bowls. Pour the dissolved gelatine into one of these quarts of wine. Dissolve the tannic acid in the other. Pour the wine containing the dissolved gelatine back into the large container and shake or stir thoroughly. When this is done, pour back the wine containing the tannic acid and stir or shake thoroughly again. The wine will become cloudy. Wipe the mouth of the container dry with a clean cloth, replace the water-valve, and put the container back on its shelf. It should be left undisturbed until it is clear and bright, which should be by the end of a month, after which it is racked anew.

FILTRATION

Although fining is the traditional and unexceptionable method of clarifying wine which will not clear by settling alone, there are other ways of doing it. One of these is by the use of centrifuges; they " settle " the suspended matter by increasing the force of gravity and throwing out the suspended matter, which has a slightly greater density than the wine in which it is suspended. This method is not wholly satisfactory, and in any case it is applicable only to large-scale wine-making.

The other, and more important, method is that of filtering the wine: that is, passing the troubled wine through a porous wall or membrane so that the solid matter is left behind and the wine emerges clear, bright, and pure. It goes without saying that the use of filters is stoutly opposed by the traditionalists. They say — what is quite true — that the *grands crus* are *grands crus* without benefit of filter, and also that filtration removes much of the wine's bouquet, adds unpleasant tastes derived from the filter, and generally transforms what might become good wine into a very sorry substance. One need not be a blind and unthinking advocate of progress to question these contentions: the test, after all, is in the tasting. If an unpleasant taste is added to the wine it must be laid to a badly constructed filter or to the improper use of a filter; for, in principle, filtration and fining are identical. In fining, a net is allowed to settle through the wine, dragging the impurities with it; in filtration the wine is allowed to settle through the net, leaving the impurities behind.

As a matter of fact, proper filtration not only clears wine more perfectly than fining, but renders it more nearly sterile, and hence more free of the threat of disease. Its only drawback lies in the cost of the equipment — a drawback which, needless to say, effectively keeps amateur wine-makers from using it, unless a group combine and buy one jointly. However, for the sake of completeness, a word or two ought to be said about the different types of filters which are used.

Wine is never filtered in contact with the air — that is, through an ordinary funnel lined with filter paper or through filtering bags. This method is very slow, and the wine is exposed too much to the air.

The filters used for wine are, therefore, all of the type which filters the wine out of contact with the air. Those most frequently used are: (1) plate filters; and (2) filters using, instead of a plate, a pure fibrous cellulose packing, which is usually called *filtermasse*.

A plate filter, reduced to its simplest terms, is simply a grill which supports a piece of filter paper or of filter cloth, the whole being enclosed in an air-tight case. The wine enters through a tap on the top under pressure (pump or gravity), passes through the filtering medium, and emerges out of another tap at the bottom, clear and bright. Such plate filters are usually adjustable in capacity: the capacity may be increased by the addition of more plates; by means of ingenious design these are so arranged that each plate works simultaneously as a separate unit, though the inlet for turbid wine and the outlet for clear wine are common to all of the plates. When filter cloth is used instead of paper, it is usual to mix an inert substance, such as powdered asbestos, with the wine to be filtered; this is deposited on the cloth and thus forms the filtering medium.

In the filtermasse filters a packing of cellulose takes the place of the plate. The filtermasse may be washed and used over and over again. Filters of this type are made as unit filters, or as multiple-unit filters of adjustable capacity. It is the filtermasse filter which was most popular in the alley breweries prior to the legalization of beer. The affluent wine-maker, or group of wine-makers, may buy a small filter of this type for as little as twenty-five dollars. Those made of iron or aluminum should be avoided. Those made of cast bronze are best.

But the amateur wine-maker need not grieve because he has no filter. Neither have the proprietors of Château Margaux or of Schloss Johannisberg.

CHILLING AND PASTEURIZATION

There remain two more practices in connection with the care of wines which ought to be mentioned, though more for the sake of completeness than for any practical value to the person who is making wine in modest quantities for his own use. One is that of *chilling;* the other, of *pasteurization.*

Chilling. Under certain circumstances wines are chilled, in the presence of air, for the purpose of speeding the process of aging. When wine is cold, it has the property of absorbing a great deal of oxygen, which in turn oxidizes certain substances in the wines and causes them to precipitate. Consequently, if the wine is chilled, say, to 40° F., and then racked in the presence of air, an effect similar to that of aging is achieved. But this practice can be used only with great caution and only when the wine is perfectly healthy.

Chilling may also contribute to the partial sterilization of wine. When wine is chilled below 50° F., fermentation ceases altogether, carbon dioxide ceases to rise, and the yeasts sink to the bottom. Also the precipitation of cream of tartar is increased, since this is less soluble in wine at low temperatures than at high; and in the course of precipitation it drags down impurities with it. Many wine-makers, in the making of white wine especially, store their wines in cellars which are never above 50° F. as soon as the secondary fermentation is finished. At this temperature wine may be kept to great age.

Pasteurization. This is the one absolutely certain and harmless method of destroying all trace of the micro-organisms which exist to some extent in every wine, healthy and unhealthy. A wine which has been pasteurized out of contact with the air, and which thereafter has no contact with the air, can never develop disease, for the reason that it contains no live organisms of disease. A temperature of 140° F. (60° C.) maintained for ten minutes is sufficient to kill the harmful bacteria.

There are several points to remember about pasteurization. One is that unless the temperature is very carefully and accurately controlled, the taste of the wine is apt to be altered, to its disadvantage; it acquires the *gout de cuit*, which every gourmet makes a point of recognizing and denouncing. Another objection lies in the fact, no longer open to doubt, that the harmful bacteria actually play an important role in the development of a wine's bouquet. Many of the harmful bacteria encourage the formation of volatile acids, in small quantity when the wine is sound, and in large quantity when the wine is definitely pathological. It is the action of these volatile acids on the alcohols of the wine which produce slowly and in small quantities the aromatic substances which give the wine its bouquet. If the harmful bacteria are entirely eliminated, by pasteurization, the volatile acids are not formed, and consequently the wine does not fully develop its bouquet.

However valid these objections may be, the fact is that pasteurization is being adopted ever more widely by commercial wine-makers, even the makers of fine wines.

Commercially, wine is pasteurized either in bulk or in the sealed bottles. The latter only is feasible for the amateur wine-maker, and even this is hardly worth the trouble. The procedure is to place the filled bottles, corked and tied, in a wire basket; the basket is inserted in a container, which is filled with water to the neck of the bottles. The water should be heated gradually, so that the temperature of the wine may be brought up gradually with it. It *must not* be allowed to exceed 140° F.; this temperature should be maintained for ten minutes, in order that there be no doubt about the thoroughness of the pasteurization.

BOTTLING

The task of bottling has a certain quality of finality about it which makes it exceedingly pleasant work. The knowledge that the wine has been brought safely through the crisis of birth and the dangers of its youth, and that it is about to come of age, yields a very real satisfaction. Every farmer knows this satisfaction also, and it is that which he celebrates with feasts of Thanksgiving when the crops have been gathered. The wine-maker can choose no better time for his bottling than the eve of Thanksgiving — always provided, of course, that the weather is propitious.

The precise time to bottle depends partly on the whim of the wine-maker, also on the character of the wine. No wine should be bottled until it is at least a year old. The reason for this is that a year is frequently required for the completion of the slow, thorough secondary fermentation. This continues very gently all winter, starts afresh with the warm weather in the spring, and often works spasmodically during the hot weather of the summer. If the wine is bottled before this, a renewal of fermentation is apt to cloud it in the bottles, to blow out the corks, and to throw down a large quantity of sediment in the bottle. Wine should not be bottled until it has lived through a summer.

And frequently one year in the large packages is not enough. A wine that is rich in tannin and high in

231]

acidity must be given more time, in order that the excess of tannin and cream of tartar may be thrown off before it is sealed in bottles. Commercial wine-makers differ greatly in the amount of time which they allow for aging before they bottle; but it is practically never less than two years, and often three or four. This allows a thorough mellowing of the youthful harshness, and a development of the maximum bouquet consistent with health. Few wines are improved by more than four years in the large package. White wines do not require as much aging as red. Few of them are improved by more than a year and a half in the large package.

It is a mistake, however, to suppose that a wine ceases entirely to mature and becomes static in bottles. A certain amount of oxygen goes into the bottles in solution, and it continues its work of gradual oxidation; and cream of tartar continues to be deposited throughout the life of the wine, still further reducing its harshness. The colour of old red wines is always attenuated, and the bottles always have sediment.

Equipment for Bottling. Bottling requires wine-bottles, wine-corks, siphon, and (though this is not absolutely necessary) a corking-machine.

Bottles. Always use wine-bottles. For white wines use white, green, or brown bottles; for red wines, dark-green. These may be bought new from any bottling supply-house, or second-hand from a dealer in second-hand glass. Let the classified index to the telephone directory be your guide. Second-hand bottles are just as good and considerably cheaper. Beer-bottles and ginger-ale bottles do not take wine-corks, and besides there is something peculiarly depressing about pouring wine from a ginger-ale bottle; but they

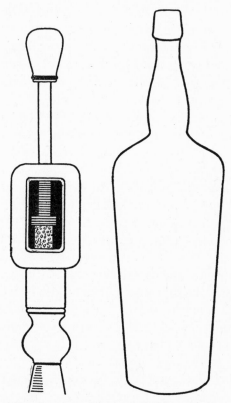

Corking-machine and Wine-bottle

will do, in a pinch, for ordinary wines which are to be served in a decanter.

Corks. The corks should be first-quality No. 9 one

233]

and one-half inch straight wine-corks. A bad cork is always a source of trouble: it may leak, and it often breaks when the corkscrew is turned into it later, causing great irritation and embarrassment. The corks may usually be bought where the bottles are bought; if they are not in stock, the bottle-dealer will order them or tell where they may be bought.

Siphon. This is the same red rubber tube that is used for racking.

Corking-machine. Corking-machines vary greatly in price, but most of them are constructed on the order of the one illustrated. A good one may be bought for a dollar.

Procedure. Never bottle except on a clear, bright day. The wine to be bottled should be completely fermented, so that there are no lingering traces of sugar to start trouble after it has been corked and put away. The wine should also be perfectly clear and bright. Some even recommend giving it an extra fining and racking two weeks prior to bottling. This is perhaps a little over-meticulous unless the wine is very choice indeed.

The bottles should be perfectly clean. They should be soaked for several hours in a solution of washing soda (an old-fashioned wash-boiler is ideal for this purpose), washed with a bottle-brush, and rinsed thoroughly. A small contraption which is attached to the water-faucet and which throws a stream of water into the bottle when the bottle is pressed down upon it speeds the rinsing tremendously. It costs very little.

THE CARE OF WINES

The bottles may be boiled after rinsing, but that is not really necessary.

When the bottles have been cleaned, they are lined up conveniently on floor or table and filled from the siphon so that the wine comes just into the neck of each bottle. The flow from the siphon may be controlled by kinking it over the second finger. Take great care not to disturb any sediment which may be in the container from which the wine is being taken. All of the wine in a container should be racked at one time; otherwise a large air space is left in it, and souring may set in.

The corks should be boiled well in advance of the time they are used; the water in which they are boiled, which discolours, should be drained off and fresh water added. They are kept soaking in this, in a closed pan. Just before they are used, they should be wrapped in a hot, moist towel. If they are boiled just prior to their use, they are so soft that they cannot be driven in satisfactorily.

Corking itself is very simple and easy. Sit down and place a bottle on the floor between your legs. Pull back the plunger of the corking-machine as far as it will go; place a cork in the chamber; place the corker directly over the mouth of the bottle; and push down the plunger firmly, driving the cork well home. It should be driven just flush with the rim of the bottle-mouth. If one has no corker, the corks must be started by hand, held in place with one hand, and pushed in with the heel of the other. The last half-inch has to be

235]

driven in with the butt-end of an ice-pick, a potato-masher, or some other blunt instrument. The corker is recommended.

The corked bottles should be left standing upright a couple of days in order to allow the corks to harden. As a precaution against deterioration of the corks, they may be sealed. A good mixture for this purpose is one part of bees-wax to four parts of rosin. These are melted together in a saucepan, and the mouth of the bottle is dipped into the mixture. Colour the sealing-wax to suit your fancy.

With bottling, the task of wine-making is finished. The bottles should be binned on their sides, so that the cork is constantly moist and the air bubble is in the middle of the bottle. The cellar should be dark, cool, and of even temperature. Unfortunately the nature of urban life makes such a cellar something to strive for rather than something to achieve. The storage place should, at least, be as cool and dark as possible and subject to the least possible fluctuation in temperature.

Chapter Nine

FALSE WINES AND SICK WINES

ONE of the facts which mankind has never been wholly willing to accept is the very stubborn one that a limited quantity of grapes will not yield a limitless quantity of wine. This fact has always been particularly exasperating in years when disease, bad weather, or other afflictions of human or cosmic origin have cut short the crop of wine grapes. Also, those who are overly stimulated by the profit motive have tended to look upon this great natural law as no more than a hurdle over which, with the help of the chemist, they have not hesitated to leap in the boldest fashion. In all wine-making countries it has been found necessary to erect a great network of legislation in order to keep the leaps of these gentlemen within the bounds of good taste. The most ardent sponsors of these laws have been the responsible wine-makers and vintners.

These projects for improving upon nature fall roughly into four groups: the rescue of sick or unsound wines either of the current vintage or of previous vintages; the manufacture of wines out of fruits other than grapes; the manufacture of wines out of

237]

the whole cloth, or, more literally, by mixing together some alcohol, water, colouring matter, and flavouring matter to produce a wine-like fluid; and that of making the grapes themselves do double — and even as much as quintuple — duty in the making of sugar wines.

SUGAR WINES

The practice of making the grapes themselves do double duty accounts for most of the false wine. Furthermore, this practice yields beverages which, if made with some little care, are so nearly like wine that they constitute a real menace to the trade of the scrupulous wine-merchant. So real is this menace that the most stringent laws are in force in every wine-making country to regulate not only the making of them, but their sale. In France their sale is absolutely forbidden, the quantities made by any wine-maker are regulated and restricted to his own domestic use, and even the quantities of sugar which may be bought by inhabitants of wine-growing regions during the vintage season are kept closely under control. These regulations are in force, not because of anything intrinsically harmful about the sugar wines, but because they are so dangerously like real wines.

Several persons in the middle of the nineteenth century, when the oidium and the phylloxera were ravaging the vineyards of France, found themselves unable to forget the fact that ordinary water and sugar are the predominant substances in grape juice, and that everything else constitutes less than three per cent of the total. A good deal of this material which is neither water nor sugar (they reasoned) must be thrown away with the skins at the pressing. It was no great flight of reason from that premiss to the conclusion that by adding sugar and water to the pressed skins a new fermentation would begin and a wine-like beverage would be produced in the course of time.

The honour of being the first to experiment in a serious way with these sugar wines, or *vins sucre*, or *vins de deuxième cuvée* as they are sometimes more elegantly called, was M. Petiot, an eminent proprietor of Bourgogne. Here are his own words: [1]

" At the vintage of 1854 I was fully convinced that one may at least double the quantity of wine by adding sugar-water to the must or husks equal to the quantity of grapes. . . . I commenced my experiments, and found the results surpass my expectations. Of a quantity of grapes that by way of ordinary procedure would probably not have given more than 60 hectolitres of wine, I received 285 — almost five times more. . . . The wine produced by the aid of sugar-water was less acid, and had more flavor (bouquet) than the natural wine; in short, it was better."

From this the conclusion seems almost inevitable that the eminent M. Petiot lacked something of the discrimination which one might expect in the *propriétaire d'un vignoble de Bourgogne*. But the story of the way in which this extraordinary gentleman

[1] Quoted by Haraszthy: *Grape Culture, Wines and Wine-making*, p. 283.

quintupled his yield of wine does not lack a certain sensational quality, even though we may be inclined to doubt the richness of the product.

A certain quantity of black grapes was crushed and pressed, and yielded forty-five hectolitres of *white-wine* must.

M. Petiot then added a quantity of sugar solution to the marc which was equivalent to the must which he had pressed. He allowed this to ferment on the skins for three days, drawing off a full quota of *red wine*, which he allowed to finish fermenting in wood.

The marc then received a new quantity of sugar solution equal to that which he had just pressed. This was fermented, and pressed free.

The marc was then required to go to work for a third time.

Then he put it to work a fourth time.

Not content with that, he then returned to his original white-wine must, which had been fermenting quietly all this while, and filled a number of kegs half-full of it. These half-filled kegs were then filled the rest of the way with fresh sugar solution, which, of course, began immediately to ferment.

Thus from one batch of grapes this audacious gentleman got twice the normal quantity of white wine, plus red wine to the amount of nearly four times what he might have had if he had originally made red wine in the orthodox fashion from his grapes. He does admit that some of the red wine from the later fermentings was pretty pallid. But this did not deter him, for, inflamed by his phenomenal dexterity, he went himself many times better, making, on one occasion, nine times the quantity that nature had expected those grapes to yield. I have no idea what happened, eventually, to M. Petiot; for he could only have carried his experiments to their logical conclusion by undertaking to supply wine for all of France from the fruit of one vine, thus making applicable in the field of œnology the theme of that dismal ditty of the nineties, " For I'm the Only Oyster Working Here." Indeed, for a while it began to look as though this slightly nightmarish conclusion were actually the goal. The practice was introduced into Germany by no less a person than the General Secretary of the Agricultural Society of Rhenish Prussia. The method was given some scientific standing by Dr. L. Gall, of Treves, and M. Chaptal, and even the great chemist Mauméné investigated it. Of more practical importance, the demand for sugar among wine-makers increased by leaps and bounds. In 1885 the wine-makers of France used 7,933,887 kilos, in the following year, 27,856,592 kilos.[1]

M. Petiot's experiments, in short, aroused a good deal of excitement among wine-makers; and though he carried the notion well toward its ultimate absurdity, he did demonstrate beyond question that a drinkable, if not particularly distinguished, wine may be produced by applying his principle with circumspection and moderation. Such sugar wines, particularly if they are made from grapes of good quality which are high in acidity and have plenty of tannin,

[1] Sadtler: *Industrial Organic Chemistry*, p. 231.

are often better than genuine wines which are made from inferior fruit. Thudichum and Dupré [1] in their great English work on wines and wine-making have this to say about sugar wines:

" The amount of acidity or of tartrate of potash in them is less than in the natural wines. The circumstance that they contain so little tartrate makes them much more like old wines, for it is well known that wines by age deposit their tartar and become milder to the taste. The infusion [sugar] wines resemble natural wines in all essential qualities; they contain all the essential ingredients, and almost in the same proportions, as the natural product. The non-essential ingredients, or those which are frequently hurtful to the natural wines, are diminished in the infused wines to such an extent that their absence is a favourable circumstance. The method promises to increase the quantity of cheap beverage and affords to the less opulent classes the means of making for themselves a cheap, wholesome beverage, even from grapes from which wines could not be obtained fit for commerce or transport."

Vast quantities of these factitious wines are made by the peasants of France for their own consumption, in order that their true growths may go into the market, a circumstance which has its parallel among American dairy-farmers, who seldom use anything but oleomargarine and condensed milk and " process " cheese. Italian wine-growers also content themselves

[1] *A Treatise on the Origin, Nature and Varieties of Wine*, by J. L. W. Thudichum and August Dupré; London, 1872; pp. 114–15.

with the fake wine. During the years of prohibition, when commerce in wines has not enjoyed the supervision of the Food and Drug Administration, it is doubtful whether a single bottle of natural wine has been drunk, save in the homes of persons who made their own wine. And even in such homes, whether of the less or the more opulent class, it is probable that a good half of the wine drunk was sugar wine. The amateur wine-maker must be very opulent indeed not to have engaged in this harmless form of cheating-at-solitaire.

Sugar Wine: Red. Red sugar wine is made from the marc which is left over after the violent fermentation, and the pressing, of the real wine. The marc is simply saved at the pressing and thrown back into the fermenting-vat as soon as the pressing is over. A sugar solution equal in quantity to the amount of wine which has been pressed is then added to the marc. The sugar-content of this solution should be twenty-two per cent, or approximately the same as the sugar-content of " normal " must. The marc which has just been pressed is of course full of yeast in its most active state, and when the sugar solution is added, this yeast immediately undertakes, once again, its function of helping the sugar to become alcohol. Within a few hours a new violent fermentation is under way; and the new sugar wine is treated from then on exactly as real wine is treated.

It is easy to estimate the amount of sugar to add to a given quantity of water to secure a solution of twenty-two per cent.

Example: Twenty gallons of wine have been pressed from the marc, and an equal quantity of sugar solution is to be added. According to the Sugar Table (page 159) 1 gal. of 22-per-cent must contains 28.16 oz. Twenty gallons would then require 563.2 oz., or 35.2 lb.

Dissolve the correct amount of pure cane or beet sugar in a small quantity of warm water. Then add to the marc in the vat about one-half of the estimated quantity of water needed, follow this with the dissolved sugar, mix thoroughly, and add the rest of the water. When the entire mixture is on the marc, it should be stirred thoroughly for several minutes. This not only assures an even distribution of the sugar, but aerates the mixture thoroughly and thus helps the yeasts to make a vigorous attack.

If the local water-supply is pretty good, ordinary tap water may be used; otherwise use distilled water. Care should be taken that the water is not too cold when it is added; the chill should be taken off first, as the action of the yeasts is otherwise slowed down.

The quality of the sugar wine may be improved considerably by bringing its acidity up to that of the original wine. Sugar wines have roughly half the acidity of the original wine. Assume that the acidity of the original wine is 9 grammes per litre expressed in tartaric acid. The correct dosage is then 4.5 grammes of pure tartaric acid per litre of must.[1] The tartaric acid should be dissolved in a small quantity

[1] 1 litre = .2642 gal.

of warm water before adding, and then thoroughly mixed.

If these directions are followed, the resulting beverage will be found to be a quite satisfactory substitute for the true wine. It has good colour, and it is drinkable much sooner than the real wine,[1] usually by the spring following its " vintage." Do not try to follow M. Petiot into the higher flights of multiplication; the results will be disappointing.

Sugar Wine: White. The making of white sugar wine differs from the making of red just to the extent that the making of real white wine differs from the making of real red wine.

When the grapes for white wine have been crushed and pressed, the left-over marc is thrown into an open barrel or fermenting-vat. To this marc is added a solution of twenty-two per cent sugar in water, in quantity about equal to the amount of fresh juice which has been pressed from the grapes.

The sugar solution is thoroughly stirred with the grapes and is left on them for twenty-four hours. At the end of that time it is pressed, and from then on, this false must is treated as though it were real must. It will be found that the fermentation is more vigorous at first in the sugar wine than in the true wine, thanks to the opportunity which it has had during the twenty-four hours of absorbing the yeast from the skins. The solution should not be left on the skins for more than twenty-four hours; if it is, it is apt to be-

[1] Thus one has something to drink while the real wine is aging.

gin active fermentation and to acquire an unpleasant brownish colour.

The acidity of the must may be adjusted in the same fashion as that described in the making of red sugar wine. It is the part of caution, also, to add tannin to the must of white sugar wine, since, as we have said, white wine musts are always deficient in tannin. Add one gramme of tannic acid for every five gallons of must. The tannic acid should be dissolved in a little warm water before adding, and mixed thoroughly.

OTHER FALSE WINES

The process which brought fame to M. Petiot, and which has just been discussed at some length, is merely the least obnoxious of the many ways of faking wines. The ingenuity which has been lavished upon the falsification of wine is positively awe-inspiring. In Greece it has so long been the custom to hide the flavour of badly made wines with pitch that the flavour of pitch is now definitely demanded. The vogue of spiced wines among the Romans had a sufficiently satisfactory explanation in their crude methods of fermentation. And the whole range of the pharmacopœia has been drawn upon at different times for such uses. Shand [1] gives the following list of chemicals " most commonly employed ": " alum, borax, acetate of lead, bi-carbonate of potash, carbonate of soda, chalk, glycerine, barium, srontium, boric acid, sul-

[1] *A Book of Other Wines than French*, by P. Morton Shand, p. xxviii.

phuric acid, salicylic acid, tartaric acid, nitric acid, copper, zinc, salt, sugar, saccharine, molasses, glucose, cider, perry, and, most common, if least deleterious of all — water." A little further on he observes that in colouring or improving the colour of wine, " brazil-wood, cochineal, cassis, cherries, elderberries, myrtle-berries, blackberries, mulberries, beetroot, fig-juice, indigo, and divers chemicals are used." He gives also receipts for an " old " Rhine wine that is made out of " 3 kilos of cider, 1 kilo of brandy, and 8 grammes of azotic ether," and mentions the notorious " Elbe " sherries, which had tartaric acid and bicarbonate of soda as their sole flavouring ingredients.

Certain of the chemicals which he mentions have, as we have seen, their legitimate uses, since they add no substance to the wine or must which is not already there naturally. Yet, even eliminating these, his list errs on the side of conservatism, it has to be confessed.

Fruit Wines. Alcoholic beverages that are made out of other fruits than grapes are commonly used in the making of false wines. Cider, particularly, is used for this in vast quantities. Sometimes the cider is allowed to ferment in its own fashion, with the help of its own yeasts, then given a synthetic white-wine bouquet when it is done. Sometimes the fermentation is stopped by pasteurization and is then begun with starters of selected white wine (usually Rhine wine) yeasts. Labounoux and Touchard in their handbook on cider [1] observe that " Germany makes, especially in the regions around Frankfurt, ciders for the export

[1] *Le Cidre*, by P. Labounoux and P. Touchard.

trade, both still and sparkling, and the latter are especially designed for competition with our champagnes," and, later: " The Germans make quantities of apple wine. They start the cider must with wine yeasts and they get a cider which faintly recalls *vin blanc*." But lest one gain the impression from these patriots that such falsifications are entirely confined to the Germans, it ought to be observed that their own provinces of Normandy, Brittany, Maine, and Picardy are sometimes involved in the same trade.

It is a pity that honest cider should thus be forced to sail under false colours, for cider, properly made from proper apples, is well able to march under its own pennon and is not at all justly characterized by Burton's observation [1] that ciders " are windy drinks." Saintsbury, indeed, who doesn't agree with Burton either, was convinced that cider apples " furnish one of the most cogent arguments to prove that Providence had the production of alcoholic liquors directly in its eye "; and he confessed that he had had ciders in his cellar, " often in bottle and once or twice in cask." In the United States the art of cider-making is much better understood by the country people than that of making wine. The bucolic tipple was left untouched by prohibition.

Perry also, which is the fermented must of the pear, is used a good deal as a basis for false wines.

Then there are the innumerable raisin wines, of which there has been a surfeit during prohibition.

[1] Burton out of Saintsbury.

False Wines and Sick Wines

Here is one receipt which I take from a recent American cookbook: [1]

Sherry Wine

6 lbs raw rice	3 gals. warm water
6 lbs raisins	1½ cakes Fleischmann's yeast
6 lbs sugar	

Put the rice and raisins through a meat-chopper and place, with sugar, in a wooden tub or stone crock. Pour in the warm water, add the yeast, which has been dissolved in a little lukewarm water, and stir all together. . . .

Sherry wine!

During the great phylloxera depression in France, *vin de raisin sec* was manufactured and sold in large quantities. One of the receipts most commonly used for concocting this mixture was the following:

White sugar	5	kilos
Raisins	5	kilos
Common salt	125	grammes
Tartaric acid	200	grammes
Common brandy	12	litres
River water	95	litres
Gall-nuts (bruised)	20	grammes
Brewer's yeast	200	grammes

And " to make this wine of a red colour it is necessary only to add to the above ingredients two hundred and fifty to three hundred grammes of dry picked hollyhocks, taking care to keep them at the bottom of the cask."

[1] *The National Cookbook*, by Sheila Hibben. Harper.

One way to get some notion of the number and variety of chemical operations which are used for making wines in a factory or for doctoring those of dubious diagnosis is to glance over the list of entries under " Fermentation Industries " in that monument to scientific diligence, *Chemical Abstracts*. In one volume there is a discussion of the use of hexamethylene-tetramine as an adulterant, a discussion of the use of hydromel (dilute fermented honey) as an adulterant, and of two methods of " improving " wine by subjecting it to ultra-violet rays and Hertzian waves. Electro-therapy is the basis of as much quackery and half-baked experimentation in treating diseased wines as it is in medicine.

Methods of killing all bacterial life by the use of noxious and dangerous substances in dangerous concentrations are not uncommon. One of the drugs most frequently found, and always watched for by official fraud-detection bureaus, is salicylic acid, a powerful antiseptic which is also highly valued for the removal of corns and warts and is used industrially as a basis for certain dyes. Boric acid is frequently used for the same purpose; indeed, every one of the American wines submitted for competition at the Paris Exposition of 1900 contained boric acid, though in very small quantities. Another drug that is used for the same purpose is sodium benzoate. Its use as a food-preservative in very small quantities is allowed in the United States. In wine-making it is used, illegitimately, to arrest acetic-acid fermentation. One of the big concentrate companies, operating during prohibition with the help of loans from the Government, regularly used and recommended it.

Mr. Shand's list of colouring and flavouring ingredients is far from complete. The extract of colouring matter from the grapes, called œnocyanin, has been available commercially for many years. An essential oil, known to the trade as cognac oil, is extracted from the lees of wine and used to give a fictitious bouquet to false wines. This oil, in its undiluted condition, has what is described as " a benumbing odor . . . disagreeable and nauseating," but in very dilute concentrations it is quite pleasant. Another source of fake flavouring matter is the vine-leaf. According to Perold, " the leaves to a certain extent possess the characteristic bouquet of the wine, and industry has succeeded in making from the leaves preparations which, when added to a wine, give it a bouquet similar to that of the wine made from the grapes of the variety which had had its leaves used in making the extract." White wines may be given a rich amber colour by the addition of caramel, such as is used for colouring gravy in cheap restaurants. A number of aniline dyes are very popular for the intensification of the wine's colour; fortunately they may be detected by quite simple tests.

Concentrates. It would be ungrateful indeed to cast aspersion upon concentrate wines, for if the concentrate has been properly made and the fermentation has been undertaken with some care, they are not bad. Furthermore, as a French paper observed in a recent issue, while speculating about the post-prohibition American wine market, these concentrates have at least served the purpose " *d'empêcher la population d'oublier le goût du vin même approximatif.*" The concentrate-making industry has only sprung into prominence during the last two or three years. The two methods most commonly used are quite different. The method favoured in California is that of evaporating the fresh juice. The unfermented must is placed in vacuum pans, a gentle heat is applied, and under the influence of the vacuum the must is quickly concentrated. One of the great difficulties encountered in this method was the fact that the volatile constituents of the fresh juice were evaporated along with the water. This difficulty was finally overcome by redistilling the water which was evaporated, recovering the smell in liquid form, and pouring it back into the concentrate. The concentrate was then pasteurized and canned.

The other method, which is not yet so popular, but is gaining considerable headway, is that of freezing out the water. The fresh juice is placed in ice-making machines, where, as it is constantly agitated, the water freezes to the side of the machine, finally leaving the concentrated juice in a pool in the middle. By this method the character of the juice is much less altered, but the same degree of concentration cannot be attained.

The concentrate is converted into a wine-like fluid by adding water until it is brought back to its original consistency, and then fermenting, either relying upon such yeasts as are present in the air or by using starters of selected yeast. The usual procedure is to buy concentrates from " servicing " companies which do the entire job right on through to the bottling, capping, and labelling. Many of the labels are very attractive. The cost of such wine is about ten times the cost of real wine made at home. It is also possible to buy the concentrate in the bulk and do the diluting and fermenting oneself. Concentrates have been much used by city-dwelling Italians who lack the space to conduct true wine-making operations.

The European wine-making nations were not slow to discover the American market for concentrates. A complete assortment of Italian wines, red and white, dry and sweet, may be obtained in concentrate form. It is even possible to get the concentrate of Pinot grapes imported from France. One is at liberty to doubt, however, that this is unadulterated Pinot.

SICK WINES

It would be pleasant to be able to approach the painful question of sick wines with a brisk and cheerful bedside manner, bringing assurance that there is nothing to worry about, that it is only a temporary indisposition after all, and that one need only give the patient plenty of rest and a pink pill every half-hour.

Unfortunately, a wine which falls ill is usually very ill indeed and presently dies, while the doctor looks on helplessly wringing his hands. One cannot emphasize too strongly that the only medical treatment that is worthy of real consideration is prophylaxis — the exercise of scrupulous care in the making, of constant vigilance in the keeping. The way to be sure of good wine is to give it a sound and vigorous fermentation in the beginning and to preserve it from infection ever after.

Pasteur demonstrated that most of the diseases of wine arise from the presence of microscopic organisms, organisms which find in wine a favourable environment for their growth and reproduction, which draw upon the wine for their food, and, in the course of their life-cycle, give off substances which destroy their host. These organisms are present, in great numbers, on the skins of the grapes at the time of fermentation. If the temperature is properly controlled, and the *saccharomyces* are granted an opportunity for development, these bad organisms are denied the chance to do their work and sink to the bottom, where they lie inert and, for the nonce, helpless in the lees. If the must has too little sugar and yields a wine low in alcohol, or if the must has too much sugar and yields a wine in which unfermented sugar remains, then the bad organisms are particularly to be feared.

In large cellars the presence of disease is ordinarily confirmed in two ways: with the microscope, and by the measurement of volatile acidity. As was observed in Chapter vii, the presence of more than .6 gramme per litre of volatile acid (as sulphuric) means that the wine is seriously sick. For the modest wine-maker two simpler tests for disease are sufficient. One is the testimony of the nose; the other that of the eyes. If a wine which has previously been unmistakably healthy suddenly develops a distinctly unpleasant smell, disease is probably present. If a wine which was clear becomes clouded, it *may* be sick — though it may also be upset only temporarily, by a disturbance of the lees, by a slight renewal of fermentation, or by one of several other causes. If it is not sick, it will presently clear again of its own accord.

Acetic Fermentation. The disease to be feared above all others — a disease which all wine-makers become familiar with and learn to abhor — is that of acetic fermentation. Its presence in any appreciable degree is instantly apparent, for its end product is vinegar — and wine which has been touched by this disease always has the sharp and penetrating odour of that useful household commodity. Mere " sourness " is not a sign of acetic fermentation, for it may only be what is called the greenness of a young wine that is still strong in unprecipitated cream of tartar.

Acetic fermentation is caused by a number of small yeast-like organisms, of which *mycoderma aceti* is most to be feared. This is the principal foe of all wine-makers. It is found normally on the skins, being deposited there from the air, but if the fermentation is properly conducted, it causes little trouble; it is also deposited on wine which is exposed to the air. It is reproduced by fission; and once its development is well started, nothing short of sterilization of the wine by pasteurization can get rid of it. This, of course, does not eliminate the acetic acid which has already been made, but merely prevents further development of the organism. *Mycoderma aceti* is a catalyst, like

255]

yeast; it affects, however, not the sugar in the must, but the alcohol which has already developed, causing that to oxidize into acetic acid. *The organism can only carry on its work in the presence of air.*

Acetic fermentation may begin at any time in the life of the wine if the wine is exposed for any considerable time to the air, but it is especially to be feared during the course of fermentation and when the wine is still young and active.

During the fermentation of red wine, *mycoderma aceti* is liable to develop on the cap of the fermenting mass if fermentation is slow and fitful, or if no space is left in the fermenting-vat in which a layer of carbon dioxide gas may form, or if the cap is not broken up regularly. If the cap is touched by acetic (and the sharp smell of vinegar will tell you), it is imperative that the top layer of skins be removed before the new wine is pressed.

But acetic fermentation gets its start most frequently during the secondary fermentation. If the new wine is fermenting slowly in wood, it evaporates, as we have seen, leaving an air space in the top of the cask in which the acetic ferments may develop; that is why constant filling of the cask is necessary. The use of glass, of course, eliminates this hazard. Acetic fermentation may be started also during this period by a failure to use water-valves, or by a failure to use a clean stopper in keg or bottle.

Acetic fermentation may be started by racking wine into a container which has " soured " from previous wine and has not been properly cleaned.

False Wines and Sick Wines

Acetic fermentation sometimes starts during the summer if the wine has not been racked, thanks to the renewed activity which the warm temperature brings to the lees.

Acetic fermentation does best in weak solutions of alcohol — that is, in wines of less than eight per cent alcohol. It is not able to work in wines of sixteen per cent alcohol or higher.

The foregoing paragraphs carry with them their own imperatives for prevention.

If the wine, through some carelessness or inattention, becomes badly tainted, there is nothing to do but allow it to turn itself completely into vinegar. This it does only too willingly; but if the quantity is fairly small, there is no need to feel bad, for wine vinegar is a luxury which every cook appreciates.

If the wine is only very faintly touched, it can sometimes be rescued by treating with *neutral potassium tartrate* (not to be confused with cream of tartar, which is *potassium bitartrate* or *acid potassium tartrate*). Neutral potassium tartrate is little used in American pharmaceutical practice and is therefore only to be obtained at the best drug stores. A dose of eight grammes of the salt to every five gallons of wine is dissolved thoroughly in a small quantity of the wine. It is then poured into the container and mixed thoroughly and left to settle for two or three days. The wine is then tasted, and if the taint has disappeared no further dosing is necessary; or dosing may be repeated if necessary as many as five times (total of forty grammes per five gallons). If it still tastes of acetic acid, then it is too far gone to be worth any more trouble. The dosing may be tried experimentally on a small quantity of the wine, using quantities of the salt which are proportionately smaller.

The use of this salt is not harmful, since it combines with the acetic acid of the wine to form potassium acetate and cream of tartar, which are precipitated. But it is a dubious remedy, nevertheless. It only removes the symptom — that is, the acetic acid which has already been formed. It does not get rid of the *mycoderma aceti*, so that if the corrected wine is not used very speedily it will be tainted again. Since part of the alcohol has already been eliminated by the formation into acetic acid, the normal balance of the wine has already been upset and the elimination of the acetic acid cannot really set it right. The use of this chemical is absolutely forbidden in France. The treatment is here included merely because amateur winemakers who have a batch of badly touched wine on their hands do not rest until they have discovered and tried the " cure." One trial, however, usually convinces them that the cured wine, though it may be drunk without unduly disagreeable sensations, is maimed for ever.

Amateurs sometimes say that they can remove acetic acid by the addition of calcium carbonate (powdered chalk). It is useless to try this remedy. It fails to remove the acetic acid, and in addition it leaves behind a disagreeable chalky taste.

Flowers of Wine. There is another ferment, much less dangerous and troublesome than the acetic ferment, which develops on the surface of wine which is exposed to the air. This is the organism called *myco-derma vini*, or flowers of wine. At first it is seen as small greyish-white points or specks floating on the surface, which gradually multiply until the wine is covered by a thick scum. This ferment, like that of acetic fermentation, will oxidize the alcohol of the wine, but unlike the *mycoderma aceti* it does not stop with oxidation into acetic acid, but carries the process to a finish, forming carbon dioxide and water. Conse-quently the wine which is seriously subject to this disease does not sour, but merely becomes flat and watery.

The flowers develop and carry on their destructive work in the presence of air; the cure for the disease is very simple and easy. It is merely to remove the sur-face growth. The simplest way to do this is to plunge a glass tube or funnel below the surface of the wine, and through this to pour more wine of the same kind into the container. The level within the container is thus raised, and the flowers are floated out through the bung-hole or mouth.

Sometimes, far from being dangerous, this disease is actually benign; and the makers of certain types of wines, notably sherries and the wines of Arbois, en-courage its growth. The distinctive characteristics of these wines are in some way, the exact nature of which is not clearly understood, owing to the presence of *mycoderma vini*. The growth of the disease is encour-aged in the making of the Arbois wines by leaving the wine on ullage — that is, by not keeping the casks filled — and for some reason the flowers develop and the acetic germ does not. When the flowers on the surface grow thick enough, the acetic germ, of course, cannot reach the surface of the wine. In the sherry country the casks of the new wine are left lying about without even bungs, in order to encourage the growth of the disease; a good deal of the wine goes acetic, but the sherry-makers consider that the wine which develops flowers satisfactorily is sufficient compensation for the loss. This curious subject is discussed at some length by H. Warner Allen in his book: *The Romance of Wine*.

Other Bacterial Diseases. In the chapters dealing with fermentation a good deal of stress was laid on the importance of keeping the temperature within certain defined limits. There is a large assortment of dangerous organisms which develop best at high temperatures, temperatures at which the fermenting power of the *saccharomyces* begins definitely to wane. These harmful organisms have been studied exhaustively by bacteriologists, but there is no need to discuss them individually here. Some of them will make the wine bitter, others will make it oily and ropy, another (*maladie de la mannite*) gives it a sickish sweet-bitter taste; and there is one, called *maladie de la pousse* by the French, which earns its name from the fact that it develops a great deal of carbon dioxide, which, gathering pressure in the closed container, presently pushes out the bung and geysers the contents of the cask into the cellar; this is especially to be found in wine made from badly mildewed grapes. The mannitic disease in particular was for years the bane of the California wine-makers; and it is troublesome in all hot countries.

The common characteristic of all these diseases, aside from their partiality to high temperatures, is that they do not require the presence of air, as do *myco-derma aceti* and *mycoderma vini*, in order to repro-duce. The only defence against them, once they de-velop, is to keep the wine in as cool a place as possible and to fine and rack it; the only means of eliminating them completely is to pasteurize the wine. But if the original must is proper and the fermentation is nor-mal, they need cause no worry.

Discoloration. Wine is also subject to a number of maladies which are not caused, like those already dis-cussed, by living organisms. These the French custom-arily lump together under the term *la casse*.[1] Fre-quently, when a half-bottle of white wine is left uncorked for a day or so — sometimes if only for an hour or so — its colour darkens sensibly, it becomes cloudy, and it throws down a considerable brownish sediment. This is the commonest kind of discolora-tion, and it is caused by the existence in the wine of a diastase which, in the presence of air, oxidizes certain substances and causes the disturbance. The diastase, it has been found, is most abundantly present in wines which have been made from mildewed grapes, and it is most successful in working its transformation when the must is low in acidity and lacks tannin.

This type of discoloration is most apt to appear

[1] Most of the wine diseases have been discovered and described by the French, and their names are French.

when wines are carelessly racked, in the presence of air, or when a container is left for some time exposed to the air. That is why, after the first racking, it is the part of caution always to rack out of contact with the air. If the fruit is sound and the must is properly adjusted before fermentation, and racking is conducted with reasonable care, this discoloration will cause little trouble.

There are other forms of discoloration, in which the wine turns milky, grey, or black. These all develop in the presence of air, and most easily when the wine is deficient in acidity or lacks tannin. Remedial treatment consists of bringing the acidity to " normal," and fining with white of egg and tannin or gelatine and tannin. The presence of iron salts in the wine is responsible for some of these types of discoloration; that is why one should not use iron instruments or containers, unless they are enamelled.

Mysterious Tastes. One last word, and this gloomy recital of symptoms, diagnoses, and partial cures will be finished. Wine, if it is carelessly made, is subject to a host of mysterious and unpleasant tastes and smells, difficult to identify and impossible to get rid of. In backward regions where the wines are stored in skins, the wine ordinarily acquires a strong bouquet of goat. That particular smell is not very hard to identify. But there are others, all brought on by the use of improper containers, by carelessness and by failure to observe the cardinal rule of cleanliness, which may easily injure the wine. There is a very old story, but a pat one, about two connoisseurs who had just broached an old cask of wine and were tasting it. They lifted their glasses and examined the colour, they twirled the glasses and passed them several times beneath their noses. Finally they sipped, and rolled the wine in their mouths, reflectively. Then they swallowed.

" I taste leather," said one, after a moment.

" Not at all," said the other; " the wine has a distinct taste of iron."

Each persisted in his opinion. Finally they decided to settle the argument by racking the wine and investigating the cask. In the bottom of the cask lay a cobbler's nail.

The story is worth remembering.

Chapter Ten

LAST WORDS

THIS book came properly to its end, I suppose, with the previous chapter. But it seems a little bit uncompromising to write a book on domestic wine-making without offering at least a few remarks on the polite art of wine-tasting, even though many admirable books already exist on that subject. In addition, there are one or two observations which I should like to make on the perhaps less polite, but fully as absorbing, subject of ordinary drinking. For some strange reason this subject is always passed by in silence in books on wine.

In discussing the uses of wine, one must be careful to make several broad and fundamental distinctions. The chief distinction is that which I have just made by inference: namely, that between tasting and drinking. The French make it when, speaking of an ordinary wine, they say that it is for *consommation* and not for *dégustation*. But I shall make a triple distinction, between *tasting*, *connoisseurship*, and plain *drinking*.

The wine-taster is a professional man, a man whose

[264

profession demands the most exacting asceticism, a man who tastes much wine, but seldom drinks. He earns his living by his highly specialized and discriminating perceptions; and as the constant smoker tends to become less discriminating, and the heavy eater less fastidious, so the drinker of much wine sometimes finds the sharpness of his critical perceptions a trifle dulled. The wine-taster must regulate his whole life in such manner as to maintain unimpaired this knife-edge sensitiveness. He must not smoke a great deal, he must not be partial to curries or other strongly spiced foods, or sweets, he must keep his digestion in perfect order, he must avoid the germ of the common cold with the utmost circumspection, he must keep careful hours. For the aim of the professional wine-taster, like that of any other ascetic, is, in so far as anyone can, to escape the bondage of self. His is the duty of judging a wine objectively; his verdict must have, in so far as is possible, a universal validity. He must be able to say, not that he *likes* the wine, but that the wine is a *good* wine. There is a world of difference. If our technicians could devise standards by which the quality of wines might be measured in the laboratory as well as their chemical composition, then there would be no need for the professional wine-taster. But the laboratory, as I have already said elsewhere, cannot pass judgment upon a wine beyond a certain point; after that, only the trained taster can carry the analysis to its conclusion.

It is useless to discuss the special technique of the wine-taster, for that would involve the dragging in of a whole technical vocabulary of its own and of a technique of which I know nothing by experience. De Cassagnac contends that even with the best of training and an iron will, most persons cannot hope to become wine-tasters. He contends that the great wine-taster has a congenital aptitude for his art. " Cooks are made, roasters are born."

Just below the exalted station of the professional wine-taster — yet above, in the sense that the amateur is often ranked above the professional — lies that of the gourmet, or connoisseur — the man who looks upon wine-drinking as an æsthetic experience. His taste is disciplined and refined, but not to the point of separation from the rest of his sensory life. He is still, however, the taster rather than the drinker.[1] The

[1] Here I cannot refrain from inserting a rather extensive footnote. The true wine connoisseurs, of whom there are few, constitute a world apart from the larger world of wine-drinkers. Wine-tasting, for them, is overlaid with a most exacting ritual. In particular they make a fetish of wine which has undergone no amelioration whatever in the hands of its maker. Such reasonable practices as the adjustment of the must in regard to its sugar-content and its acidity cause them to hold up their hands in horror. Wine, they say, is a living substance, whose birth is a miracle and which goes through the cycle of growth, decline, and death as does every other living thing. To attempt, then, to interfere with this natural process — to " make " wine — is a sort of blasphemy. Since I have consistently recommended such interference, I must anticipate their criticism. To begin with, the domestic wine-maker does not have unlimited freedom to pick and choose. If he has no vines of his own, then he must depend upon what the market has to offer, and make the best of it. If he does have his own vines, he must still contend with a Nature which does not always have the best interests of the domestic

gourmet prides himself, first, upon his ability to appreciate a wine — that is, to pronounce judgment upon its quality as good, indifferent, or bad. He flatters himself, also, that he can tell pretty well its age, and that his opinion as to its possibilities for the future — whether it will improve or is already declining — is worthy of respect. He is proud, also, of his knowledge of wines — his recognition of the grapes from which it was made and his ability to distinguish roughly between the wines of the great wine districts. And finally he achieves in greater or less degree a specific knowledge of wines, so that he can tell not only a wine's particular growth or place of origin, but the year of

---

wine-maker at heart. Is he, then, stubbornly to disregard proved methods of amelioration — when, if he does, his wine may be foredoomed to inferiority? It seems rather foolish. A wine that is free from disease, that is sound and potable and refreshing — though it cannot hope to be a *vin de luxe* — is better, I think, than wine that is just plain bad.

And there is another reason for disregarding the living-substance argument. It does not hold water even when the premiss is granted. Let us agree, as they insist, that wine is a living substance which is born, grows to maturity, and eventually dies. What better argument could there be for bringing science to its assistance? We know full well what medical science has already done to prolong and improve the quality of human life. The wine-maker who adopts enlightened practices does not " make " wine any more than an obstetrician makes babies. He does not change its essential " wineness " any more than the obstetrician changes the essential humanity of the unborn child. The obstetrician's duty is to prepare the way for the unborn child and to do his utmost to bring it safely into the world; he thus at least partly assures the child a healthy life. The intelligent pre-natal care of wine seems to me to be every bit as reasonable and legitimate.

its making as well. We may say in regard to this last gift especially that it is often boasted, but seldom attained. Among the inhabitants of the United States there are few such gourmets, for the reason that such knowledge is acquired only by long experience and faithful study, and a limitless assortment of wines is a without-which-no. It is safe to say that even among those who speak openly and confidently of their knowledge and their gifts in this regard, not one is qualified beyond a very limited range. The thoughtful host does not question the self-announced connoisseur, but he is careful to drop some word beforehand as to the wine or wines to be served. Indeed, it is an unwritten rule among connoisseurs of wine, who, after all, have as much need for preserving their *amour propre* as the rest of us, never to serve a wine or to let it be served unannounced; that would be as distressing as the refusal of a musician to announce his encore. To commit a vinous deception is as serious a breach of good taste as to commit a literary hoax.

True connoisseurs surround their use of wine with many niceties, some of which I offer here not so much from a conviction of their overwhelming importance as from a sense of duty. There are first the many — and very perplexing — problems connected with the preparation of wines for the table. Doubtless every wine from every grape of each different year and every vineyard is shown to its best advantage at a specific temperature — though even that temperature would doubtless change from year to year, as the wine "develops" with age. But not even the connoisseur has yet reached the point of deciding upon these temperatures. He contents himself with generalizations. Thus, a red wine, other things being equal, shows itself best at " room " temperature, and a white wine parades its virtues most effectively at a temperature somewhat lower. Mr. T. Earle Welby, whose opinion on such questions is not to be taken lightly, contended with great vigour and show of learning that the ideal temperature for a red wine is 65° F., neither more nor less, and that the accepted practice of " chilling " a white wine, by immersion in ice or crudely placing it in an electric refrigerator, is open to the gravest suspicion. There are ways and ways of bringing a wine to its desirable temperature. It is manifestly disturbing to the wine to bring it from cellar temperature to " room " temperature by popping it for a moment in an oven or a pail of hot water, as it is manifestly wrong to use crude ice for the cooling of white. If red wine, the bottles must be brought from the cool cellar at least three hours before the meal, so that the wine may accustom itself gradually to the temperature of the dining-room.[1] As for the manner of cooling white wine, the bottle must first be " wrapped in a cloth wetted with cold water and stood for a while in a draught; and then, when the wine has gradually declined in temperature, a cloth wetted with a mixture of tap water and the water from melting ice has been substituted for the first cloth. The wine has not been

[1] But Mr. Welby insists that the wine should under no circumstances reach room temperature sooner than a half-hour before the beginning of the meal.

shocked, and it has not been brought down more than a few degrees below cellar temperature — say to between 48 and 50 degrees."

But there is more to the preparation of a wine than the attainment of the proper temperature. Red wines, if they have been in bottle for any length of time, invariably have a sediment, which has settled in a streak along the under side of the bottle as it lay in the bin. The manner of avoiding the inconvenience and distress which might be caused by this sediment splits œnophiles wide apart into two schools — the school of the decanter and the school of the bottle.

One school contends, with Mr. P. Morton Shand, that " a decanted wine inevitably leaves something of its body and soul behind it in its old home. It is far better to sacrifice a third of the bottle." It is not, of course, actually wasted, for what is left may go to the kitchen for cooking. Those who think as Mr. Shand does bring the bottles to the dining-room for warming well before the meal and stand them on the sideboard on their bottoms; thus gradually the sediment which had accumulated along the side of the bottle slips to the bottom, leaving the wine clear and free to be poured without muddying. It is of course necessary, once the cork has been drawn and the bottle tilted for pouring, to keep it tilted, otherwise the swishing of the wine will disturb the lees and render the wine, for purposes of connoisseurship, worthless.

The contenders for decanting claim that their method avoids the waste of wine, assures its absolute clarity, and gives the wine a chance to " breathe " before it is tasted. Just before the meal is to be served (the bottles having been standing for several hours), our host draws the cork [1] and grasps the upright bottle by two fingers at the neck. In the other hand he holds a decanter, which has been gently warmed to receive the wine. Standing before a light — candle or electric bulb — he tilts the bottle and pours the wine slowly into the decanter. As he pours, the sediment slowly creeps toward the mouth of the bottle; just before it goes over the lip, he stops pouring. If he does his decanting skilfully, he need not lose more than a half-wineglass of wine. Still a further refinement which some favour is that of pouring it through a silver funnel which has been packed with cotton wool. But this is used only for very old wines bearing a great deal of sediment.

Once the wine has been prepared for the table, there is still the question — filled with pitfalls for all but the connoisseur — of the proper glass. Briefly, the requirements for a good wineglass are that it shall display the wine to best advantage, that it shall provide the wine a proper opportunity to develop its bouquet, and that it shall be large enough. As for the first of these qualities, the worst pitfall is fairly obvious. The glasses should not be colored. A wineglass of ruby or green may deserve and receive the connoisseur's admiration as an example of the glass-blower's art, but he will pour no wine into it. The colour of a wine is one of its most

[1] Good corkscrews are not easy to find. Usually the " screw " is too short.

271]

agreeable properties, and one capable of the most subtle variation; it should be clear to everyone — but isn't, apparently — that red wine in a green glass ruins the appearance of both for all save the colour-blind, and that red wine in a ruby glass is redundant. I say this with full knowledge that some of Mr. George Washington's wineglasses were red.[1] Uncoloured glass, then, and as thin and clear as possible, should be the rule; a glass with elaborate etching upon it distracts attention from the wine itself. As for the second requirement — that the glass shall allow the wine to develop its bouquet (if it has any) — there has never been an improvement over the tulip-shaped type, the glass whose bowl comes in a little at the top, for the effect of these converging walls is to concentrate the bouquet rather than to disperse it. Much ingenuity has been lavished on the design of department-store wineglasses — to little effect, so far as the œnophile is concerned. The glasses should also be of generous size. The so-called claret glass of the marts of trade holds hardly more than two mouthfuls, and if the glass is only two-thirds filled, as it ought to be, that means only one and one-half mouthfuls to the pouring. Finally, the wineglasses should have stems; they enable one to lift and twirl and admire the wine without smudging the bowl with finger-prints. The notion that the most expensive glasses are the best is false; almost the reverse is true. Very simple, clear white glasses of satisfactory size and fairly good shape, suit-

[1] Despite prohibition, these have remained on display in that glorious junk-pile the National Museum, Washington, D. C.

able for either white wine or red, may be bought for as little as $3.50 the dozen.

One might go on indefinitely describing the travail which a connoisseur goes through in preparing his wines for the dinner. But we must pass to other things. There is still to be considered the manner of tasting. Let us say, then, that our connoisseur has his guests seated about him. It is time for the tasting of the great wine of the evening. The food is simple, but of course perfectly prepared. The preliminary wines have been agreeable, but not great — charming preludes, rather, to the masterpiece. With proper solemnity, relieved, perhaps, by an appropriate anecdote, the host has announced the wine, has drawn the cork, and after pouring out a quarter-glass for himself (to make sure that none of his guests shall suffer the indignity of a chance grain of cork) has, let us say, himself poured the wine for his guests. What shall the connoisseur guest do? Pick up his glass, between remarks to his neighbour, and toss it off? Horrors! No. There is a very elegant story that is used by all connoisseurs to illustrate the correct approach. I bow to tradition, and repeat it, though I cannot lay claim to connoisseurship. My version is that which is given by de Cassagnac, who protests that all other versions are inaccurate:

" One day when M. de Talleyrand was giving a dinner, an admirable *fine champagne* brandy was produced. The man speaking to M. de Talleyrand took his glass and drank it down at a gulp. Talleyrand, who was a great gourmet, could not, despite his extreme courtesy, refrain from an exclamation. The guest perceived that he had obviously committed a breach of good manners.

"'What have I done, monseigneur?'

"'Well, sir, since you ask me, let me tell you that a fine champagne of that age and quality deserves to be appreciated.'

"'Doubtless, monseigneur, but I am one of the un-initiated.'

"'Well, sir, one can learn. . . .'

"'With pleasure, monseigneur. Would you vouch-safe to instil the first rudiments?'

"'Willingly,' replied Talleyrand. 'Thus: one takes one's glass in the hollow of one's hand, one warms it, one shakes it and gives it at the same time a circular movement, so that the liqueur may liberate its scent. Then one lifts it to one's nose, one breathes it in —'

"'And then, monseigneur?'

"'And then, sir, one puts one's glass down and — talks about it. . . .'"

M. de Talleyrand's advice (though he was speaking of brandy and not of wine) makes clear in the most vivid manner the great gulf which lies between tasting and mere drinking. Actually, though, it is very literally the " first rudiments." The connoisseur first lifts his glass to the light, to a candle preferably, in order that he may admire and comment upon its colour. If he detects any foreign bodies in the wine, he is politely non-committal, thus expressing his disapproval with-out giving any grounds for the accusation of rudeness. Then he follows de Talleyrand's advice and twirls it a while, in order to bring out its bouquet, and lifts it to his nose. This allows him immediately to detect odours which should not be there, as the odour from a bad keg, that derived from a faulty cork, a trace of acetic acid, and so on. If he detects any of these, he is at liberty to lift his eyebrows a trifle or to continue to be elaborately non-committal. But if the wine is all that the host thinks it to be, this first experience of the bouquet is very delightful. It invites repetition, and the connoisseur passes the glass several times beneath his nose and perhaps re-examines its robe of colour, at last bringing it to his lips. The time for the actual tasting has arrived! The host glances anxiously from face to face, awaiting the verdict. The taster has taken a generous mouthful, which he does not swallow immediately, but holds in his mouth. He swishes it around, as decorously as may be, allowing it to flow beneath his tongue, to strike the roof of his mouth — in order that every taste bud shall have its chance at it. Simultaneously he breathes out through his nose, in such fashion that the bouquet may penetrate to the last corner of the cavities of his head. Then the wine is swallowed, the swallowing sensation being followed quickly by that faint and delicious warming of the stomach and a pervasive sense of well-being, and the aftertaste, which is a sort of " sense " of cleanness and freshness in the mouth which is quite indescribable. For some moments after the tasting, no word is spoken. The host, in an agony of anticipation, continues to glance from face to face. The assembled gourmets, on the other hand, have no eye for the host. Their eyes rest on a shadow, or are fixed absently upon some object in the centre of the table; they have turned in upon themselves, intent on the analysis of their own sensations. Then, finally, the oldest connoisseur present breaks the silence. " Jove! " he cries. " How shall I ever repay you for that experience? " The host assumes a pleased, a coy, or an I-told-you-so expression, according to his disposition, as one by one the others add their words of praise. The table has broken into animated conversation, as the tasters compare their sensations, and parade their vocabulary of wine-slang and grasp of œnopoetics generally.

And that is the way wine is tasted.

2

That is the way wine is tasted, but it is not quite the whole story, for our gourmet must not only see that the wine is properly prepared for the experience, but must prepare himself as well. Good health and a hearty appetite are the first requisites, but they are not enough. Our gourmet, if he knows that fine wines are in prospect, will have abstained from smoking for several hours before the dinner; for it is one of the minor tragedies of life that these two delights, smoking and wine-tasting, cancel each other out. Tobacco dulls the taste buds to such an extent that immediately after or during smoking it is practically impossible to distinguish a fine wine from an ordinary one. The host who declines to serve fine wines to a man who smokes between courses does not consider that he has committed a breach of good manners, for he assumes that by smoking his guest has indicated that he would just as soon have ordinary wine anyway. The other great pre-dinner enemies of wine-tasting are highly flavoured appetizers, whether liquid (cocktails) or solid (canapé). These so astonish and stun the taste buds that those delicate organs do not recover for a long time. Such appetizers are useful only when wine of dubious quality (from the point of view of the connoisseur) is being served.

This point about appetizers leads logically to a consideration (though it will be brief) of the whole question of the relation of food to wine — a subject of endless fascination, and one over which all gourmets argue endlessly. Needless to say, the food which is served at a wine-tasting dinner is chosen with the most exacting care and is faultlessly prepared. Yet the food is distinctly subordinate to the particular wines which the host desires to serve. This is a reversal of the customary method, by which the menu is first arranged and the wines are then chosen with reference to the courses which have been decided upon. The typical wine-tasting dinner is therefore relatively simple, consisting of an hors-d'œuvre or soup, an entrée, a roast or poultry or game, with a vegetable, and cheese.

The custom used to be to serve with the hors-d'œuvre or soup a dry sherry or Madeira; but the world of gourmets has concluded, on impeccable grounds, that this is unwise. For such wines have the grave disadvantage that they assert themselves too well, so that the memory of them is apt to clash or jar with the more delicate wines to follow. Connoisseurs, then, are more and more discarding hors-d'œuvres, save oysters or melon. With oysters a light dry white wine goes very nicely; with melon, no wine at all. With soup, wines are hardly necessary, though if it is a bisque a light white wine may prove pleasant, especially if other white wine of the same general type is to follow. Frequently both soup and hors-d'œuvre are dispensed with, their places being taken merely by green olives, which prepare most admirably for every sort of wine.

It is with the entrée that the wine-tasting properly begins. But the character of the wine which the host wishes to serve at this point will determine the character of the entrée. With light dry white wines, such as Rhine wines, white Burgundies (Chablis, Montrachet), and so on, an entrée in which cheese has been used goes very well. With somewhat sweeter white wines a fish entrée may be served; but here there are many opportunities for error. It is distinctly dangerous to have any of the fishier fish, such as mackerel; and it is important to avoid highly flavoured (and themselves delicious) sauces which contain vinegar, capers, and so on. Vinegar is the uncompromising enemy of all wine. A plain hollandaise sauce is excellent. A grilled fillet is excellent too. One other pitfall is to be avoided; and that is the pitfall of the egg. The egg, for all its glorious virtues, was not meant to accompany serious wine-tasting. The entrée which is predominantly egg is therefore to be avoided, unless its flavour is masked with cheese.

And now for the meat — and, usually, red wine.

For red wines, whether light or full-bodied, nothing is better than a roast of beef. But grills are excellent, and so is a plain roast chicken or fowl, and so are the game-birds. Veal, on the other hand, supports a white wine well. Roast duck has no place in a wine-tasting dinner, if the lighter clarets and Burgundies are to be served; it demands a red wine of much fortitude and aggressiveness if the quality of the wine is not to be lost entirely.

As for the vegetables, these are neither helpful nor detrimental, though the carrot is to be avoided on account of its sweetness (which will kill a light dry red wine). Greens are only suitable with dry wines.

The finest red wine is often reserved for the cheese; for cheese is a most satisfying accompaniment to any wine. Camembert, Roquefort, Brie, Stilton — some one of these is to be found in every wine-tasting dinner that is worthy of the name. Cheese is, as de Cassagnac says, "the interpreter of all wines, and if one dare say so, their touchstone. It admits all wines, exalts all wines, whatever they be; or underlines their deficiencies."

If there be a dessert, it always follows the cheese, which is properly a part of the meal itself, and with sweets there can be only a sweet wine.

3

Finally, one or two things ought to be said concerning ordinary wine-drinking. For the domestic wine-maker is concerned much less with fine wines than with the wines called ordinary, the wines which stand at the basis of the pyramid and whose freshness and utter lack of subtlety have their own peculiar charm and in the end, perhaps, wear better. The domestic wine-maker may occasionally surprise himself with a wine of very exceptional character — a wine bearing a tantalizing and unique fragrance, a wine of which the qualities are so felicitously blended, so justly balanced, that it announces itself at once as something above the common run. But those are the exceptions rather than the rule, and the domestic wine-maker will be unwise to count on them, at least during his novitiate.

In the plain wine-drinking household the choice of wine is distinctly subordinate to the choice of food. In most such homes, especially the more humble ones, there is but one wine of current consumption, usually a red wine from one of the cheaper grapes — say, Alicante Bouschet or Zinfandel. Then there is no question of choice at all. The wine consumed is Alicante Bouschet or Zinfandel, whether the meal be Saturday left-overs or the Sunday roast. Choice first enters when a white wine — say, a Delaware, or a Thompson's Seedless or a Catawba — joins the red in the cellar. The plain and useful red remains, of course, the basis of the family's wine-drinking; but for fish or a veal roast or cold chicken or many a " made dish " a bottle of the white wine may be brought forth. And for cooling it the ice-box is plenty good enough; no need to bother with damp cloths and draughts. In the wine-drinker's home there are always a couple of bottles of red wine on the pantry shelf and a bottle of white wine in the ice-box. The appearance at the table of one or the other is as regular as the appearance of bread.

When the domestic wine-maker adds other varieties of wine to his cellar, he may begin to experiment with the fitting of various wines to various foods; and great fun it is. He will find that his Delaware or Catawba goes perfectly with oysters; that a California Petite Sirah is glorious with duck, being well able to hold its own; that few things are more satisfying to the hungry man than a vast heap of spaghetti, prepared as it ought to be with meat and mushrooms and many other things, and washed down with a great deal of rude and homely Alicante; that steak with mushrooms and a fat decanter of Colonel Haraszthy's Zinfandel are ideal companions; and that a joint of Chicago beef has unsuspected glories accompanied by a Norton. He will discover that plain food is capable of the most surprising exaltation by good domestic wines. And before long, perhaps, he will begin to understand the wisdom of that pleasant old gentleman who explained his vigorous old age by saying that every day since he could remember he had drunk a bottle of good wine, except when he did not feel well, and then he had drunk two.

GRAPE DISTRICTS OF THE UNITED STATES

There is very little in this book about American viticulture, as distinct from wine-making. That is because our viticultural literature is quite voluminous already. The best book for the person who would grow his own grapes, as well as make his own wine, is Hedrick's *Manual of American Grape Growing*, and the next best book is Munson's *Foundations of Grape Culture*. In addition the bulletins and pamphlets of the Federal Government are available, not to mention the excellent series published by the State of California and the State of New York. Adequate information is also to be found in any number of gardening handbooks. Nevertheless, it has seemed to me worth while to include this brief catalogue of the viticultural possibilities of the various parts of the country. I have omitted from the lists many excellent eating varieties. The map and much of the information given below are adapted — a polite synonym for lifted — from *Grape Districts and Varieties in the United States,* by George C. Husmann (U. S. Depart-

283]

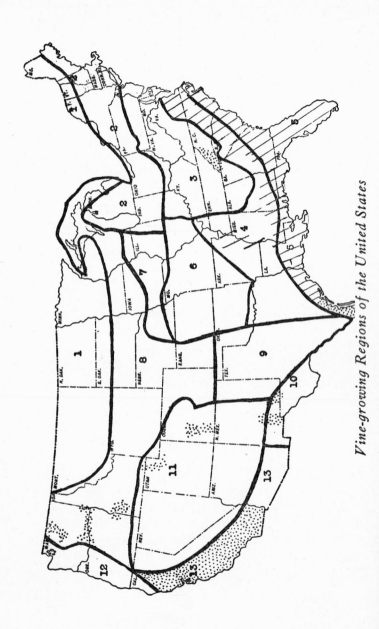

Vine-growing Regions of the United States

ment of Agriculture Farmers' Bulletin No. 1689), which is to be had from the Superintendent of Documents, Washington, D. C., for the price of five cents.

The division of the United States into thirteen viticultural districts is fairly arbitrary, and the lines dividing them are not to be taken too literally. Then, too, conditions vary tremendously within each district. The northwestern part of Montana, say, does not very much resemble the northernmost point of Maine; yet they are both included in District No. 1. The lists of grape varieties given below are, however, fairly dependable.

District No. 1

This district extends nearly all the way across the northern United States. Its winter temperatures are apt to kill the vines, and the short growing-season keeps most varieties from ripening. Consequently only the hardiest varieties, not much good for wine-making, may be grown with any chance of success. Those recommended are Alpha, Beta, Dakota, Hungarian, Janesville, Monitor, and Suelter.

District No. 2

This is the best of the native-grape districts. It includes the Finger Lake, Ontario, Chautauqua, and Michigan regions and is nearly everywhere suited to the growing of good wine grapes. *White-wine varieties:* Brighton, Catawba, Delaware, Diamond, Elvira, Iona, Salem. *Red-wine varieties:* Bacchus, Clevener, Clinton, Concord, Eumelan, Ives.

District No. 3

It is impossible to offer any generalities about soil and climatic conditions in this district. But in practically every part certain varieties of native grapes may be grown very successfully. The growing-season is generally somewhat longer than that of District No. 2. *White-wine varieties:* Brighton, Catawba, Delaware, Diamond, Elvira, Iona, Rommel, Salem. *Red-wine varieties:* Bacchus, Clevener, Clinton, Concord, Cynthiana, Ives, Lenoir, Norton.

District No. 4

The growing-season of this district is longer still, but many parts of it present serious disease difficulties. The *rotundifolia* grapes — Scuppernong, Flowers, and the rest — are indigenous to those parts which are covered with slanting lines. As for the other varieties, they are: *White-wine varieties:* Brighton, Delaware, Diamond, Elvira, Noah, Rommel. *Red-wine varieties:* Concord, Cynthiana, Herbemont, Lenoir, Norton.

District No. 5

This is predominantly the district of the *rotundifolia* grapes and, in Florida, of the grapes belonging to the species *munsoniana*. These are admirably resistant to the grape diseases which thrive in hot, moist regions. However, a few varieties of other species may be grown. *White-wine varieties:* Delaware, Hidalgo, Noah. *Red-wine varieties:* Beacon, Herbemont, Lenoir. When grafted on native stocks and given careful cultivation, *vinifera* varieties may also be grown in some parts of this region.

District No. 6

This district produced many of the best wines prior to prohibition, and there are still large vineyards in many parts of it, especially in Missouri and Arkansas. *White-wine varieties:* Brighton, Catawba, Delaware, Diamond, Dutchess, Elvira, Grein Golden, Missouri Riesling, Noah, Rommel, Salem. *Red-wine varieties:* Bacchus, Clevener, Clinton, Cynthiana, Eumelan, Lenoir, Norton.

District No. 7

Winters in this district are fairly severe, but the growing-season is sufficiently long for many varieties. *White-wine varieties:* Brighton, Delaware, Diamond, Elvira. *Red-wine varieties:* Bacchus, Concord, Clinton, Ives.

District No. 8

This vast and heterogeneous district embraces many soils and much variation in temperature. In general, it is not particularly well adapted to grape-growing, although the hardier varieties usually succeed, and in some favoured spots grapes do very well indeed. In those portions which are dotted on the map, *vinifera* varieties may be grown, with irrigation and winter covering. Eastern portion: *white-wine:* Delaware, Diamond, Elvira; *red-wine:* Bacchus, Concord,

Ives, Lenoir. Western portion: *white-wine:* Delaware, Diamond; *red-wine:* Concord, Ives.

District No. 9

This district, consisting largely of the western part of Texas, is not particularly well adapted to grape-growing. The following varieties are recommended for trial: *white-wine:* Delaware, Hidalgo, Rommel. *Red-wine:* Herbemont, Lenoir.

District No. 10

Where irrigation is possible, in the Rio Grande and Pecos valleys, and in the El Paso section, the *vinifera* varieties do very well. Those grown are principally Sultanina, Mission, and Muscat, but there is no harm in trying some of the better wine varieties.

District No. 11

The mountainous parts of this district are naturally out of the question for grape-growing; but in the valley some of the hardy varieties succeed. *White-wine:* Brighton, Delaware, Diamond. *Red-wine:* Bacchus, Concord, Ives. In the irrigated regions (and the amount of land under irrigation continues to increase) which are free from alkali, it is possible to grow the hardier *vinifera* varieties, such as Sylvaner and Zinfandel.

District No. 12

Vinifera varieties are grown in the dotted parts of this district. Husmann recommends, however, the growing of native American varieties. *White-wine:* Brighton, Delaware, Diamond, Elvira. *Red-wine:* Bacchus, Clevener, Concord, Clinton, Eumelan, Ives.

District No. 13

It is needless to say anything about this district other than that the *vinifera* varieties thrive here.

BIBLIOGRAPHY

A selection of useful books and pamphlets relating to viticulture, wine-making, and the appreciation of wines.

AKENHEAD, D.: *Viticultural Research.* London, 1928. Empire Marketing Board, H. M. Stationery Office.

ALLEN, H. WARNER: *The Romance of Wine.* New York, 1932. Dutton.

ALLEN, J. F.: *A Practical Treatise on the Culture and Treatment of the Grape Vine.* New York, 1853.

ALWOOD, WILLIAM B.: *Enological Studies.* U. S. Department of Agriculture. *Notes on the Use of Pure Yeasts in Winemaking,* 1909, Bulletin 129; *The Sugar and Acid Content of Different Varieties of Grapes,* 1911, Bulletin 140; *The Chemical Composition of American Grapes, etc.,* 1911, Bulletin 145; *The Chemical Composition of American Grapes, etc.,* 1916, Bulletin 452.

American Type Culture Collection, Catalogue. Chicago, 1928. John McCormick Institute for Infectious Diseases.

BIGELOW, W. D.: *The Composition of American Wines.* Washington, 1900.

BIOLETTI, FREDERIC T.: *Elements of Grape Growing in California*. Berkeley, 1929. University of California, Circular 30.

BONNET, L. O.: *Enemies of the Vine*. San Francisco. California Grower.

BUTLER, FRANK HEDGES: *Wine and the Wine Lands of the World*. New York, 1926. Brentano's.

California Grower. San Francisco. Files to date.

CASSAGNAC, PAUL DE: *French Wines*. Translated by Guy Knowles. London, 1930. Chatto.

CHANCRIN, E.: *Le Vin*. 10th edition. Paris. Hachette.
—— : *Viticulture moderne*. 10th edition. Paris. Hachette.

CHAPMAN, A. CHASTON: *The Yeasts: A Chapter in Microscopical Science*. Washington, 1926. Smithsonian Institution.

Commissioner of Patents, Report, Chapters on Wine-making. Washington, 1857.

DAVIDSON, W. M., and NOUGARET, R. L.: *The Grape Phylloxera in California*. Washington, 1921. U. S. Department of Agriculture, Bulletin 903.

DOWNING, A. J.: *Fruits and Fruit Trees of America*. New York, 1860. (Many other editions also.)

EMERSON, EDWARD R.: *The Story of the Vine*. New York, 1902. Putnam.

GLADWIN, F. E.: *Grape Growing in the Eastern United States*. New York, 1931. The Rural New Yorker.

HARASZTHY, A.: *Grape Culture, Wines and Wine Making*. New York, 1862.

HARDEN, ARTHUR: *Alcoholic Fermentation*. Revised edition. London, 1932. Longmans.

HEDRICK, U. P.: *The Grapes of New York*. Albany, 1908. State of New York.

Bibliography

HEDRICK, U. P.: *Manual of American Grape Growing*. Revised edition. New York, 1924. Macmillan.

HEWITT, J. T.: *The Chemistry of Wine Making*. London, 1928. Empire Marketing Board, H. M. Stationery Office.

HILGARD, E. W.: *Report on Viticultural Work, being a part of the report of the Regents of the University*. Sacramento, 1882. (Also reports in subsequent years.)

—— : *Reports of Experiments on Methods of Fermentation*. Sacramento, 1888. University of California.

HUSMANN, GEORGE: *American Grape Growing and Wine Making*. 4th edition. New York, 1895. Orange, Judd.

HUSMANN, GEORGE C.: *Grape Districts and Varieties in the U. S.* Washington, 1932. U. S. Department of Agriculture, Bulletin 1689.

—— : *Grape Propagation, Pruning and Training*. Washington, 1932. U. S. Department of Agriculture, Bulletin 471.

—— : *Testing Phylloxera Resistant Stocks*. Washington, 1930. U. S. Department of Agriculture, Technical Bulletin 146.

JULLIEN, A.: *Topographie de tous les vignobles connus*. Paris, 1866.

MUNSON, T. V.: *Foundations of Grape Culture*. New York, 1911.

PACOTTET, PAUL: *Vinification*. Paris, 1926. Baillière.

PEIXOTTO, ERNEST: *A Bacchic Pilgrimage*. New York, 1932. Scribner.

PEROLD, A. I.: *A Treatise on Viticulture*. London, 1927. Macmillan.

Pure Wine, Hearing before the Committee on Ways and Means, 56th Congress, 1st Session. Washington, 1906. H. R. 12868.

REDDING, CYRUS: *A History and Description of Modern Wines.* London, 1851.

ROOS, L.: *Wine Making in Hot Climates.* Melbourne, 1900.

ROSE, R. SELDON: *Wine Making for the Amateur.* New Haven, 1930. Privately printed.

SAINTSBURY, GEORGE: *Notes on a Cellar Book.* London, 1927. Macmillan.

SHAND, P. MORTON: *Bacchus, or Wine Today and Tomorrow.* London.

—— : *A Book of French Wines.* New York, 1928, Knopf.

—— : *A Book of Other Wines than French.* New York, 1929. Knopf.

SHEEHAN, A. M., and others: *Juice Grape Varieties.* San Francisco, 1924. California Grower.

SIMON, ANDRÉ L.: *The Blood of the Grape.* London, 1920. Duckworth.

—— : *In Vino Veritas, a Book about Wine.* London, 1908. Richards.

SKINNER, W. W., chairman of editing committee: *Official and Tentative Methods of Analysis of the Association of Official Agricultural Chemists.* 3rd edition. "Beers, Wines and Distilled Liquors." Washington, 1930.

STERN, G. B.: *Bouquet.* New York, 1927. Knopf.

STOLL, H. F.: *Grape Districts of California.* San Francisco, 1931. California Grower.

STOLL, H. F., editor: *Official Report of the Session of*

BIBLIOGRAPHY

the International Congress of Viticulture. San Francisco, 1915.

THUDICHUM, J. L. W., and DUPRÉ, AUGUST: *A Treatise on the Origin, Nature and Varieties of Wine.* London, 1872.

United States Department of Agriculture, Annual Reports. 1862 to date.

WAIT, EUNICE: *Wines and Vines in California.* San Francisco, 1889.

WELBY, T. EARLE: *The Cellar Key.* London, 1933. Gollancz.

WILEY, H. W.: *American Wines at the Paris Exposition of 1900.* Washington, 1903.

INDEX

(Names of grape species and varieties in italics)

INDEX

iii]

Index

v]

Index

Index

ix]

Index

[x

INDEX

INDEX

A Note on the Type in which this Book is Set

This book was set on the linotype in Janson, a recutting made direct from the type cast from matrices (now in possession of the Stempel foundry, Frankfurt am Main) made by Anton Janson some time between 1660 and 1687.

Of Janson's origin nothing is known. He may have been a relative of Justus Janson, a printer of Danish birth who practised in Leipzig from 1614 to 1635. Some time between 1657 and 1668 Anton Janson, a punch-cutter and type-founder, bought from the Leipzig printer Johann Erich Hahn the type-foundry which had formerly been a part of the printing house of M. Friedrich Lankisch. Janson's types were first shown in a specimen sheet issued at Leipzig about 1675. Janson's successor, and perhaps his son-in-law, Johann Karl Edling, issued a specimen sheet of Janson types in 1689. His heirs sold the Janson matrices in Holland to Wolffgang Dietrich Erhardt, of Leipzig.

Composed, printed, and bound by The Plimpton Press, Norwood, Mass. Paper made by S. D. Warren Co., Boston.

WHITE WINE

In using this synopsis, the wine-maker should refer at each step to the appropriate part of the book.

1. *Necessary Equipment.* Crusher, 2 pails, press, 2 bags for pressing, funnel, tub, saccharometer, siphoning hose, containers for wine (preferably five-gallon bottles), absorbent cotton, clean cloths. See pp. 183, 144.
2. *Grapes.* For suitable varieties see p. 174.
3. Crush grapes into tub, press immediately, and pour fresh must into five-gallon bottles. See p. 183.
4. If making sugar wine, see p. 245 at this point.
5. Add dose of tannin. See p. 186.
6. Test must for sugar-content. See pp. 185, 155.
7. Test must for acidity (optional). See pp. 186, 159.
8. Adjust sugar-content and acidity. See pp. 185, 186.
9. Settling. See p. 188.
10. Violent fermentation, one to six weeks. See p. 189.
11. Rack new wine into clean containers. See p. 191.
12. Analysis of new wine (optional). See p. 196.
13. Secondary fermentation. See p. 213.
14. Second racking, one month after first. See p. 217.
15. Third racking, in February. See p. 220.
16. Fining, or clarification, if necessary after second racking. See p. 225.
17. Fourth racking, in June. See p. 217.
18. Fifth racking, in October. See p. 217.
19. Bottling, not before the October racking. See p. 231.